LEAD GENERATION HANDBOOK

Lead Generation Handbook

63 Ways You Might Not Have Thought Of To Get More Prospects, More Quickly, At Less Cost

Robin C. Johnston

iUniverse, Inc.
New York Lincoln Shanghai

Lead Generation Handbook
63 Ways You Might Not Have Thought Of
To Get More Prospects, More Quickly, At Less Cost

iUniverse books may be ordered through booksellers or by contacting:

iUniverse
2021 Pine Lake Road, Suite 100
Lincoln, NE 68512
www.iuniverse.com
1-800-Authors (1-800-288-4677)

ISBN-13: 978-0-595-38723-6 (pbk)
ISBN-13: 978-0-595-83104-3 (ebk)
ISBN-10: 0-595-38723-3 (pbk)
ISBN-10: 0-595-83104-4 (ebk)

Printed in the United States of America

CONTENTS

▼

Introduction

If you've purchased this book for yourself, it's a pretty safe bet that you have an interest in getting more clients or customers for your business. And no matter how well your business is doing, that's always a good interest to have.

Professional services providers rely on expanding their client base or landing repeat engagements from existing clients. Retailers depend upon customer traffic and predictable sales volume. Enterprise software sales professionals live or die by their sales pipeline and deal flow. Regardless of the business or industry you're in, if you can't find and close business, you're out of business. After all, there aren't many challenges in business that can't be solved by a steady stream of new clients, consistent retail sales, or closed deals. And we all know that tomorrow's sales depend on the prospecting we do today.

In the pages which follow you will find a collection of ideas to explore as you look to improve your lead generation process; sixty-three ideas, to be exact. Try them out. But understand from the start that not all of them will work for you. Some will be completely inappropriate, and others will need a little tinkering to fit your circumstances. Don't try and *force* these ideas to fit exactly as they are presented. Rather, experiment with them. Test them. Adapt them. Take the time to massage them and see if they can work for you. Give special consideration to those ideas that seem unusual for your type of business. That's the surest way to discover a breakthrough lead generation approach.

The purpose of this first section of the book is simply to get your creative juices flowing. If you find just one good nugget of advice in what you read here than the book has been a good investment for you.

Near the end of the book I present my "MACM" business development model. MACM—which stands for Core **M**arketing Message, Prospect **A**cquisition, Client **C**onversion, and System Performance **M**easurements—is a complete system for generating business. It's a way of breaking the business development process down into its central components, allowing you to analyze each component and find out what's working and what's not. Only by looking at business development in this way can you systematically improve your lead generation efforts and move toward consistent and predictable sales.

It's always been a mystery to me why so many otherwise smart businesspeople leave their lead generation to chance. They participate in a never-ending, desperate dance to find that next account or tap that next market. They struggle on and on, moving from one idea to another and never stopping to figure out exactly what part of their sales machinery is broken.

It doesn't have to be that way. Lead generation is a system that brings marketing and sales together into the effective business development process they were meant to be. That's what the MACM model is all about.

If you implement MACM or put any of these lead generation ideas into practice in your company, drop me a line to tell me about it. Let me know what works as well as what doesn't work, in your particular line of business. I'd love to hear from you. And I'd especially appreciate hearing about any lead generation ideas you've found that work particularly well for you. If I use your idea in a future edition of The Lead Generation Handbook, I'll send you a copy with my compliments.

If I can be of any further assistance to you in your efforts, feel free to give me a call.

Good luck on your next lead generation campaign!

Robin C. Johnston

Announce Yourself

Most local papers and many trade journals have sections for local or industry announcements. There is typically no charge to submit information for inclusion in these announcement sections. And in this day and age, few businesses can afford *not* to use any free media opportunities that present themselves. Surprisingly, however, few companies take advantage of this opportunity with any regularity.

There are real advantages to making announcements like these. When we read this sort of "public information," we often do so without using the "commercial content filter" that we usually use when we read ads. As a result, the information comes across as more factual and more credible, and therefore stands a better chance of influencing our attitudes, beliefs and values.

Look in local newspapers, Chamber of Commerce publications, customer publications, trade and regional business journals and other periodicals. Use Member News, Announcements, and other similar sections to announce hirings, contracts, expansions, etc.

Plan your announcements like you would plan a paid advertisement. Think about the desired effect you want to have on your prospects. How do you want their attitudes to change? Of course, you can't expect to get away with using the same language that you would use in an ad. What you should consider is this: "what state of mind are my prospects in when they read this publication, and how do I get their attention?"

Hint: it's not about YOU! Visibility here relies upon connecting with your audience through some mutual association with them. Can you catch their attention by referencing relevant associations, education, or other credentials? Take a look through the current listings in a few of the publications that carry these types of announcements. What catches your eye? It might be that the same information caught the eye of your prospects.

CHECK PUBLIC RECORDS

Most governments keep track of a great many things, from employment to property ownership to health records to drivers license histories. A surprisingly high proportion of this information is available to just about anyone who knows how to go through the right channels. Some, such as property tax information, is posted freely on the Internet. In other cases, Freedom of Information Acts in the U.S., Canada, and other countries require government officials to make information available upon request, with minimal bureaucratic burden.

In North Carolina, for example, the State's general statutes read:

> *"The public records and public information compiled by the agencies of North Carolina government or its subdivisions are the property of the people. Therefore, it is the policy of this State that the people may obtain copies of their public records and public information free or at minimal cost unless otherwise specifically provided by law."*

The statutes of other jurisdictions have similar provisions.

Getting access to this information is not usually complicated. It shouldn't be too much of a surprise to know that attorneys were among the first to figure this one out. Get a speeding ticket in just about any state these days and it won't be long before your mailbox sees a deluge of propositions for legal services to fight your case.

Most of this information is free. You just have to know where to look and how to request it. Start by contacting the jurisdiction that collects and controls the information you are seeking to access. Ask them what options exist for you to obtain this information, and what costs may apply for doing so.

Pay 'Em Off

How much are you willing to pay to get a new customer? For low-value, low frequency items or services in industries where there is a little loyalty and no switching costs, likely not very much. If your business doesn't match that profile, however, there is a seldom-used tactic that might be just the thing to sway some business your way.

When it comes right down to it, the root cause of most hesitation to try a new vendor is some sort of risk. Something—often risk of financial loss—holds prospects back. Instead of spending your money on sales or marketing campaigns, why not give the money you would have spent to generate leads and make sales calls directly to your key prospects, so that they can try your products or services at no cost? Eliminate the risk and you often remove the most significant barriers to trial.

To make this work, the first thing you will need to do is to calculate the lifetime value of a customer. How much does one customer spend with you over time? Next, figure out how much you can afford to spend to acquire a new prospect. With this knowledge in mind, all there is left to do is let your potential customers know what you're planning to do, and then just let them try your products or services. Send each prospect a personal letter telling them they already have an account with you, and that it contains some amount of money that they can use at any time this year.

This tactic is not common, but it is done. Some of the most popular online trading services around today use this very same tactic. They send you a letter telling you they have opened an account for you with $75 or so in it. You get the money when you do your first trade.

SET UP A FISHBOWL

The "fishbowl" technique is hardly new. For decades—maybe longer—retailers have put out a bowl with a sign attached asking customers to leave their business card in return for an opportunity to win some sort of prize. Why do they do this? The offer is not entirely altruistic.

The real idea is to collect patrons' names and addresses. Aside from building a mailing list (known in direct mail circles as a "house" list), fishbowl card collections help retailers determine and map their trading areas. This insight provides many benefits, including the ability to refine promotional targeting when using "blind" mail drops or buying outdoor ad space.

There's nothing difficult about setting up a fishbowl, and the technique doesn't need to be costly. To drive response, you will need to offer a desirable incentive. Although some "fishbowl anglers" choose items completely out of the blue, the best incentives are something related to your business. This way, the pool of prospects you develop is more likely to be semi-qualified. Typically, only those with some level of interest in what you have offered will leave their cards. Once you've decided on your offer, simply set out a container for collecting the cards, and put up a sign asking visitors to leave their card in return for a chance to win the item you've promised.

To get things started, you may wish to drop in a couple of dozen "starter" cards. Mark these cards on the back with a distinguishing mark, so that you will know to remove them as you sort through the cards you have collected at the end of your collection period.

Fishbowls are often seen in non-retailing environments as well. For example, they can be used at public events or club functions such as trade shows, Chamber of Commerce events, or civic club meetings. While fishbowls used in this way tend not to be as useful for trade area mapping, they can still serve to generate a tidy mailing list of prospects.

CREATE A HOTLINE

"Free" is a powerful motivator. Almost since the telephone first appeared, savvy marketers have been using it to offer information to prospects in expedient and cost-effective ways. One way to do this is to set up a free telephone hotline. Some hotlines play pre-recorded messages, while others use live call center operators.

There are countless examples: horoscopes, lottery numbers, weather reports, and traffic delays are just a few. Some businesses encourage prospects to call and ask questions about how to use their products, or suggest a product or service they'd like to see offered. Others allow prospects to ask questions about problems they have encountered, and offer solutions on the spot.

The main advantage of hotlines is that they let you keep in touch with your customers. Aside from staying top-of-mind, each contact gives you the chance to sell something. Because the hotline is free, the media will be more inclined to give you free publicity because of it. You can also tell reporters you'd be willing to share with them from time to time the top five questions people are asking. Information such as this is valuable to the media, because it can be a good tip off to emerging trends.

One example is the Butterball hotline. This service is designed to help even the most inept cook prepare a perfect Thanksgiving dinner. Butterball gets fabulous publicity by telling reporters about the most outlandish questions it receives such as "How do I turn on the oven?"

Implementing a lead generation program doesn't get much easier than this. Of course, the first thing you have to do is set up your hotline. Once you've got your message recorded, send a few press releases out to key influencers at radio and newspapers in the geographic areas that you target. The novelty of this idea almost always compels the media to call. If your hotline is set up to provide valuable information, the media will get the word out for you.

Give 'Em An Earful

Despite the Internet and advances in telephony, we all spend time in voice mail holding patterns every now and then. Sometimes we hear nothing but a periodic "please stay on the line" message. Sometimes we get the radio. And sometimes—just sometimes—we get offers for additional products and services for the company we are calling. Although it does nothing for prospects that aren't already calling you for one reason or another, an on-hold marketing program can dramatically lift sales of add-ons or ancillary products or services.

When developing your on-hold program, it is helpful to refer to the following simple process. Start by creating an overall outline for your program. Decide how long the entire audio loop will be, and determine how many segments will fit in that time. Keep in mind that each segment should be no longer than 30 seconds. This helps ensure that you keep listeners' interest all the way through each segment, and also increases the chance that listeners will make it through at least one entire message before the party for whom they are waiting picks up the phone.

After you have mapped out the overall program, decide what subject categories will be explored in the various segments. There are several categories you might wish to test, including:

- Product or service benefits and recommendations

- New product introductions

- Sale and promotion announcements

- Information regarding upcoming holidays or hours

Finally, count the number of words you can comfortably say in 30 seconds, and then pencil out a draft script for each segment.

The field is getting crowded with companies providing on-hold marketing services, but the leader is still Muzak (muzak.com). Best known for the adapted tracks playing in elevators everywhere, Muzak provides turnkey on-hold marketing solutions that fit nearly any budget.

STRATEGIZE FOR ORGANIC SEARCH

If you've got a presence on the Internet, you're missing the boat if you haven't geared up for organic search. Although there are more "sophisticated" ways to divert search traffic to your site, the vast majority of search-initiated leads come from this more pedestrian approach.

The terms "organic" or "natural" search refer to the traditional practice of search engines "spidering" pages and returning to fill their indexes with data. Regardless of how well you're doing with your other traffic driving activities, it's worth your time to prepare for these arachnid visitors. Here are some reasons why:

> *"Online shoppers are nearly three times more likely to find what they want on the Web by using search engines versus responding to advertisements."*
>
> —WorldPay

> *"According to Google, more than 55 billion searches were conducted on their search engine alone during 2002 and nearly 80 million searches 'of a commercial nature' are being conducted each day."*

It would be much too ambitious to try and lay out all of the details of how to prepare for organic search here. However, the following are some "Do's" and "Dont's" that will help you take care of the basics and steer clear of some of the common trouble areas.

- Use Meta Tags: Both Description *and* Keyword tags

- Use Page Titles

- Use IMG ALT Tags

- Use Flash Pages Sparingly

- Include Keywords in Site Content

- Avoid Frames

- Get Listed in the Open Directory

- Get Other Sites to Link to You

- Don't Use Redirects

- Don't Hide Keyword Text

Plan a Blitzkrieg

Blitzkrieg is the German word for "Lightning Strike". This is a concentrated period of intense and continued attack directed toward a specific objective. In business, that objective is usually a burst of sales resulting from an extraordinary number of customer contacts made in a short time period.

An effective blitzkrieg can develop as many leads as would normally take months to develop. Not only can this add a much-welcomed shot of revenue, but it serves as a tremendous motivating force to recharge and realign discouraged sales team members.

Good planning is essential for a sales blitzkrieg. Determine exactly what is to be accomplished by the attack, who is to be contacted, what interested prospects need to do next, and how long the blitz will last. Measure your success, and compare results of everyone making blitzkrieg sales calls. Also be sure to track results from campaign to campaign, and create a benchmark that you can use to estimate the value of future blitzkrieg campaigns.

The best way to ensure a successful campaign is to build your blitzkrieg around a strong hook or message. Tie your call in with a new product or service offering, store opening, sale, or other special event. If there are more people than just you calling, motivate your team by providing incentives for developing certain numbers of leads or reaching pre-determined sales volumes.

Help Their Fingers Do
the Walking

For some businesses, there's simply no better way to get in front of prospective buyers than through that time-tested shoppers guide, the Yellow Pages. If yours is the type of business that consumers typically search for in this grand-daddy of all business directories, it would be a horrific mistake not to be there.

There are few other media that offer the pre-qualification afforded by the Yellow Pages. People do not usually look through these huge volumes unless they are looking for providers of a specific product or service. Therefore, you can be reasonably well assured that callers have at least a superficial interest in what you have to offer.

But being there and being the first one that prospective buyers call are two different things. It takes more than a good page position to be the one that breaks through the cacophony of ads and compels buyers to call you.

If you've got to be in the book, follow these key tips:

Choose size over color—As larger ads usually out-pull smaller, colorful ones, spend any extra money on the increasing the size of your ad

Hit hot buttons—Use a bold headline in your ad that focuses on your customers' key benefit

Sell everything, and be thorough—List all products and services you have to offer, referencing brand names, where possible. Also, make it easy to contact you by providing your full address, phone numbers, and web site.

Finally, never reference your Yellow Page ad in your advertising. In driving potential customers to your Yellow Pages ad, you put them directly in front of your competitors' ads, as well, making it easy and virtually encouraging customers to shop around.

Run a Classified Ad

You may never have bought anything after reading a classified business ad, but that doesn't mean they don't work. *Somebody* buys from them, or they wouldn't have enjoyed the success that they do, and been able to command so much space in major daily newspapers, year after year after year.

Classified advertising is commonly divided into four categories: real estate, automotive, recruitment, and general public advertising.

There is a self-qualifying aspect to classified advertising. Specifically, most people who take the time to read through the listings are in the mood to buy, and are looking for a way to satisfy a current need or want. Therefore, most people who respond to your classified ad will have a genuine interest in what you have to offer.

The key to making classifieds work for you is testing. Test everything about your ads; publications, category placement, headlines, the offer, and your call to action.

The headline is by far the most important aspect, and is estimated to account for as much as 70% of the success of any ad. Make sure your headline is bold and that it relates to your prospects' most pressing need or problem. Remember that most people who read classifieds do so in the hopes that they will be able to satisfy a current need or problem. What matters most to them? What do you have to say to get their attention, and lead them to read your ad instead of the ones before or after it?

People who read classified ads tend to screen out ads they have seen more than two or three times in a period of time. To offset this, you should adopt a practice of devising a few different ads for each offer, and rotating them every couple of days. You will stand a better chance of getting through to ad skimmers with your message.

Join a Leads Group

How many times have you heard someone ask, "Do you know a good attorney? Dentist? Accountant? Chiropractor?" It happens all the time. For just this reason, a number of groups have emerged to keep professionals and business owners in contact with one another, and stimulate the exchange of leads.

Most professional leads groups will only accept one member from each industry or professional group. For example, an optometrist who belongs to a leads group can be assured that he/she is the only optometrist in that particular chapter or club. This prevents conflicts from occurring when a member brings a lead to a group where two or more people provide the same product or service.

The format of most leads group meetings is similar. There is typically a welcome by the club president or other executive officer, followed by 30-second or 1-minute "mini-commercials" given by each member. Then there is a slightly longer "program," during which one member does a more detailed introduction to their business, and explains the type of lead that would be best for him/her. Sometime during the meeting, leads are formally passed to members using pre-printed lead sheets.

There are several leads groups that have grown to international proportion, and boast hundreds of chapters with thousands of members. Some of the more popular leads groups include Business Network International (bni.com) and LeTip (letip.com).

A benefit of joining a well-organized group like this is that, if you travel for business, you can often contact chapter presidents for the cities you are visiting, and arrange to attend as a guest. Provided that what you offer can be sold to people in this new area, this lets you extend your trading area into new regions.

ADVERTISE IN A
CARD DECK

A card deck is a package of advertisements enclosed in an envelope, and sent out to hundreds, thousands, or even millions of businesses or consumers. Most decks are sent out on a monthly basis, but some are sent less frequently.

Perhaps the most well known of all consumer card decks, Val-Pak has been serving American marketers since 1968. There are more than 220 franchises serving regional markets in the U.S., Canada and Puerto Rico, and most people have received their blue envelopes filled with advertisements and coupons for dozens of local and national businesses.

Do these really work? Yes! If not, the whole card deck system would have shut down long ago. But they do work better for some businesses than others.

The most important thing to remember when planning a campaign is to zero in on your target market. Many decks offer opportunities to target your promotion to the neighborhood level. This gives you more control over who receives your offer, and lets you attract customers from outside your trading area, without the cost of providing discounts to your existing customer base.

Another key to using card decks effectively is to provide a strong enough incentive for prospects to take some sort of action. Don't try to sell your product or service directly, however. The objective is to get potential customers to identify their interest in what you have to offer. If you offer a "free" report on how to do something or other, and people register to receive it, you know they're a good candidate for products and services related to the subject of the report.

One last thing. People like to respond to offers in different ways, and people have different means to contact you. Therefore, your card should include as many ways as possible for prospects to contact you. Don't assume that simply providing a toll-free number is enough. List your physical address, web site and an e-mail address, too.

Play Tennis or Golf

There's something to be said for sweating it out together.

Despite golf's overwhelming popularity as the businessman or woman's game of choice, there are alternatives that can work just as well, for those who don't favor the Scottish national pastime. Tennis is a good substitute, as are squash and racquetball. The key is that you're out of the office, away from distractions, and spending time with your prospect in a friendly yet competitive environment.

What is it about these activities that make them valuable in the game of business? Some advocates say that you can tell a lot abut a person's business style by observing them at play. Others hold a more practical contention, claiming that interaction in sport brings people closer together, and makes a productive working relationship easier to attain.

Whatever the reason, there is no doubt that an investment of time on the links or on the court can pay off handsomely in business.

Look for a club that matches the style of the people with whom you would like to meet. If your potential customers are upscale, check out upscale clubs. At the same time, it is important that you are comfortable meeting and competing with your prospects, so make sure the club you choose feels right to you, too.

Go to Your Customers' Trade Shows

When you set up an exhibit at trade shows for your industry, you face the challenge of differentiating yourself from your competition. As your customers walk past row after row of vendors, differentiation tends to blur, and customers come away with a sense that there are several options that might meet their needs.

If your company sells to other businesses, try attending your *customers'* trade shows. There are several benefits to doing this. First, as few companies put forth the effort to do this, you can easily differentiate yourself by being one of the only firms to make the effort to go to meet at these venues.

You can also observe how your customers interact with their customers. Depending on what you sell, this can be valuable information indeed. And your customers will certainly recognize and appreciate your interest in helping them achieve their sales goals.

Keep in mind the reason why your customers are there in the first place. This is their opportunity to reach their own customers, and sell their own products. Therefore, it is essential to make your entry in a respectful and non-intrusive way.

The best way to do this is to make the rounds late on the opening day of the show. Your objective at this time is simply to introduce yourself and "press the flesh". Let them know why you are there, tell them that you will drop back in to see them at the end of the show, and wish them a successful show. Then get lost for a few days.

When you go back to visit the customer at the end or the show, spend the first few minutes discussing the show itself. Find out if your prospect met their objectives, and how this event compared to events at which they have exhibited in the past. This will help get you in alignment, and make your actual sales call much more productive.

Get on the Radio

We've all heard professionals and business owners on the radio discussing some aspect of their work. Doctors get air discussing new techniques in coronary surgery. Attorneys are asked to discuss the importance of wills and estate planning. And business owners are given the chance to discuss the impact of new tax rules. But have you ever stopped to wonder how they got there?

Like print media, radio stations exist to provide content for their audiences. To get high ratings, they must provide a steady stream of information of interest to those who tune in to them. One way to do this is to bring in guest "experts" to discuss topics of interest. With the right approach, you can be that expert.

The best thing about getting on the radio is instant credibility for you and your business. Most people don't understand how the broadcast media works, and automatically think that the station sought you out as a well-known expert in the field. While that can and does happen, that's not the only way to get on the air.

The truth is that it's not that difficult to get invited in to do a talk segment on the radio. One of the main reasons many people do not pursue radio programs is that they are simply afraid to try! In many cases, just the thought of being broadcast to many thousands of listeners petrifies people.

There are several types of programs on which you might appear, including general interview shows, interview/call-in shows, panel shows, and specialized programming. Topics you can address include trends, how-to information, or what's new in your industry.

To get your "fifteen minutes of fame," prepare a pitch letter to sell the producer on your idea for a radio show. Pitch letters should be as brief as possible; never more than two pages. E-mail your letter to radio station program managers and call to follow through a couple of days later. When you call focus on the story, not on the pitch letter. With a good story idea and a little tenacity, you'll get the chance to make it on the air.

Get Customer Referrals

Many people have difficulty asking existing customers for referrals. And yet, as no one knows our value better than those that have already bought from us, there isn't a better source of leads! Learning to ask for referrals effectively and consistently is an essential part of building a business.

When customers refer others to your business, your business benefits from an instant credibility boost. Like a newspaper editorial about your business, this is far more valuable than any advertising you could do for yourself.

To get referral business, start with providing excellent service. The first step is to make sure that the person you are going to ask for a referral truly believes in what you have to offer.

Once you've got an advocate, the next step is to "ground them" on the specific value you provide. Ask two questions. First, "How did everything go with the work I did for you?" Follow this with, "What were the best parts?" Suppose that the referrer says that what they really liked are *A, B, and C.* At this point, you've created a common basis of positive experience. Now simply ask, "Would you give me the names of three people who might also benefit from *A, B, and C*?" It couldn't be easier than that.

If you still can't make the ask, there are a few impersonal ways to generate customer referrals. They can range from simple "Tell-A-Friend" appeals to more sophisticated programs that track customer referrals and reward those that consistently introduce new customers to the business.

On the Internet, organized customer referral programs are also known as "viral" marketing. Like the organisms that inspired them, these campaigns proliferate very quickly, and can easily reach many times more people than might be reached with a company-directed campaign.

Enter Contests

Everyone loves a winner. And in the competitive world of business, it is not uncommon for prospects to lend winners a sort of "expert" status, simply on the ground that their product, service or organization has won some sort of award.

Expert status implies credibility. And credibility supports sales. That's why it pays for you to enter industry-related competitions. The best ones are those that you know are held in high esteem by your current and prospective customers.

You don't even need to take first place in order for this tactic to produce benefits. Even an honorable mention can draw the right kind of attention.

To get started, look for appropriate competitions in industry-related journals and web sites. Don't forget to check out your competitors' sites, as those who have won awards previously will probably be promoting their success on their home pages.

Although procedures will vary widely from contest to contest, entering is usually pretty straightforward. Simply familiarize yourself with the entry requirements, and submit your entry.

Caution is in order, mind you. Not every competition will be worth your while. And some can be downright dangerous. It is not unheard of for unscrupulous competitors to run their own contests, simply so that they can trick unsuspecting rivals into sending them what would ordinarily be confidential information.

Remember to promote <u>any</u> award you receive to your current and prospective customers. Some competitions provide a crest or seal that winners may display on their web site and marketing materials. If you win, make sure you find out if some form of recognition logo is available for you, and wear your badge proudly!

HIRE A TELEMARKETER

If you know how to get prospects to react over the telephone, consider teaching someone else how to do it, too. There's a lot to be said for tried and true. With the right tools and a little organization, a telemarketer can deliver as many as 10,000 4-minute presentations each year. That's why leading companies in a wide range of industries including financial services, home alarm-monitoring services, and long distance telecommunications continue to employ in-house telemarketing staff. We may not like to get cold called, but the simple truth is that it works! Take care to stay on the right side of the law, however. In the U.S., recent changes to federal legislation let consumers add their names to a Do Not Call list (donotcall.gov). Calling on people who have opted out can result in steep fines.

Hiring and training a telemarketer to make calls for you can free up time for you to work on other tasks. Also, once you've developed a model for teaching people how to develop leads, it is a relatively easy next step to scale the model up to produce a greater volume.

Make it as easy as possible for telemarketers to succeed. If you've found a pitch that works for you over the phone, write it down and make telemarketing staff study it and learn it word for word. Track their results, note their stumbling points and any common objections they encounter, and refine the script until it sells consistently.

Don't underestimate the commitment it takes to supervise telemarketers. Running a good telemarketing operation is not a simple matter of showing telemarketers the ropes and letting them do their thing. They need constant motivation and encouragement, and regular performance check-ups to make sure that they stay on target.

When you get to the stage of having three full-time telemarketing staff, you may want to consider hiring a dedicated telemarketing manager. Hiring, training, motivating, evaluating, and rewarding a telemarketing team takes a lot of work, and doing it effectively can easily consume more time than you had anticipated.

HAND OUT BOOKMARKS

A freelance writer in Toronto, Canada once wanted to build a business consulting to aspiring writers. He reasoned that most writers are also avid readers and, therefore, they were likely frequent patrons of that city's public libraries.

To reach them, he developed a simple yet elegant device that readers and potential writers would *want* to pick up and take with them; a bookmark.

The pieces were about 1–3/4" wide and 8" long, and printed on both sides. The "front" side made a clear pitch for the seven-week e-mail course, while the backside provided supporting testimonials, along with a brief bio of the writer.

The results were astounding! In just a couple of months, the writer grew a very large mailing list of qualified prospects, sold several subscriptions to his e-mail course, and even landed a few personal consulting engagements. The success of this simple and cost-effective device was well beyond the writer's expectations.

How can you use this in your business? Maybe you can't. That really doesn't matter. The point is that there are as many communications options as you choose to imagine, and put in place. If bookmarks don't fit your image or can't reach your intended audience, think of something that does.

Trying to reach school-age children? Create and hand out textbook covers. Do you serve a particular religious community? Sponsor a church bulletin. Need to get to computer users? Everyone needs mouse pads.

The key attribute of a good communications media is that it gets the attention of your target audience. After that, it all comes down to the message.

HIRE A LEAD
GENERATION FIRM

For a variety of reasons, it is not always feasible to set up your own tele-marketing department. Sometimes there are no staff resources available with the skills or time to manage a telemarketing effort effectively. In other cases, the need is a short-term one, and doesn't justify establishing a permanent call center. In these situations, it may make sense to hire a lead generation service.

There are thousands of firms in the U.S. alone that will make cold calls for you. These companies are known by a variety of names, including telemarketing or lead generation firms, outbound call centers, and rain-makers.

The best telemarketing services have a structured system in place to learn about your business, products and services before they start mak-ing calls. While you may be hesitant to invest in this level of prepara-tion before you see what the results could be, the results will clearly be less than they could be, with a well-prepared telemarketer on the end of the phone. Like anything else in life, preparation pays.

You also want to make sure that you engage a firm that has adequate experience in your industry. It is important that those people making the calls are familiar with your industry, its products and competitors, and that they are comfortable calling on the decision-makers that they will need to call. Ask about the ages and professional experience of the people hired as telemarketers for any business you consider working with.

Insist on weekly or semi-monthly reporting. Some agencies will provide monthly status reports, but this is usually too infrequent for you to be able to make changes to the pitch, or focus in on a different audience.

As mentioned previously, there is no shortage of lead generation companies to call. Here are a few for starters:

- Corporate Rain (corporaterain.com)

- Technology Sales Leads (tsleads.com)

- BuyerZone (buyerzone.com)

CREATE AN E-MAIL SIGNATURE

Faster than any medium before it, e-mail has become a standard for communications of all sorts. As the leading reason that most people use the Internet at all, e-mail is now firmly a part of our culture. And in the business world, it is an absolutely indispensable tool.

Most of us fire off dozens or hundreds of e-mails each day, and receive an equivalent number. And yet, a surprisingly few businesses have established a policy for the content of the e-mail signatures that many users include at the bottom of their messages.

E-mail signatures are the few lines of text that follow our name, at the end of all of our e-mail messages. They are unequalled in their ability to get a message in front of those with whom we communicate regularly. Best of all, it costs nothing to slip a message into an e-mail signature.

Here are a few pointers to help make your e-mail signatures more effective lead generation tools:

- Keep 'em Short—most people do not want to read through lines and lines of additional text, after they have read the content of your message itself. In addition, long e-mails are very discourteous to the visually impaired, and can also create problems for some e-mail clients.

- Include a Positioning Statement—all e-mail signatures should include a concise, to-the-point statement about the purpose of the business.

- Make an Offer—provide some sort of incentive to engage prospects and encourage them to make contact with you. Many organizations include a link to their web site and an offer of some reward or information.

- Use Consistent Signatures—make sure that all employees use the same e-mail signature format. An eclectic collection of e-mail signatures conveys an attitude of disorganization.

GIVE IT AWAY

Direct marketers have this one down cold. They know that one of the best ways to develop a pool of qualified prospects is to offer something for free.

We're not talking about the logo emblazoned coffee mugs or cheesy baseball caps that are forced upon us at trade shows. We're suggesting that you give away something much more potent, much more powerful: Information.

Providing information benefits the giver in a number of ways. Most notably, it is an easy way to build credibility, and gain trust. The concept is "Show, Don't Tell". Prospective clients can assess your capabilities much more readily when you show them what you can do for them than when you simply tell them.

But there's an even more important reason to give away information that can help your prospective clients. When someone downloads a report, registers for a white paper, or writes in for a free book, that's a good clue that the information relates to a present or potential future need. The very act of requesting the information qualifies your prospect as a candidate client.

The best information items to give away are white papers, reports, and practical guides on how to solve common problems. Excel spreadsheets are also popular, if your services have a quantitative element. For example, one DC-area CPA offers a series of spreadsheets that help clients in a range of areas, including estimating corporate valuations, or creating a balanced scorecard model.

You may think it impractical to give away information for which you could charge clients. Though not uncommon, this worry is unfounded. If all of the value you have to provide can be summed up in a 10-page report or spreadsheet, you probably don't have much worth selling, anyhow. On the other hand, leading prospective clients into an environment of mutual trust is the way to develop a business that bears plentiful fruit, season after season.

Join A Trade Association

As the old saying goes, "Birds of a feather flock together". Similarly, businesspeople in all industries tend to congregate with those most like them. Trade associations exist to facilitate this, and allow businesses to share information and discuss ways to address the challenges confronting their industries.

While this means that there is probably a trade association for your industry, it also means that there are also likely to be trade associations for each of your major customer groups. This presents a much greater opportunity for you in terms of lead generation.

Joining your customers' trade associations puts you right in the thick of things, when it comes to getting your customers' attention. There are many benefits. You get to know the main players in your target industries. You get an opportunity to network and bring attention to your business. And you get to learn about the full scope of challenges your customers face.

This last benefit is the most important. It is this deep level of awareness and understanding of customer problems that will set you apart from many of your competitors, equip you to answer customers' chief concerns, and establish you in your customers' eyes as someone who really has their interests at heart.

Don't be surprised to find that some trade association membership rules prohibit non-industry members. Some industry groups have been inundated with imbedded "outsiders" in the past, and are more than a little hesitant to have their members affronted by deal-hungry salespeople at every industry event.

HOLD A CONTEST

In the mid-1980s, the California Closet Company launched a national campaign to get leads. With masterful execution, the company held a series of contests to find the messiest closets in America. With the promise of a free closet design for all of the winners, homeowners were encouraged to send in pictures of their closets and storage spaces.

The contest was a massive success and generated tremendous publicity for California Closets. But that's not even the best part of the story. Even more valuable than the publicity were the hundreds of leads that streamed in from coast to coast. The company ended up with an instant mailing list of qualified homeowners who had self-identified themselves as being unhappy with their current storage arrangements. Talk about a great way to get semi-qualified leads!

The beauty of this approach is that the respondents have not only identified themselves as having a particular problem, they have also indicated a desire to fix it. This inherent needs qualification is half the battle. The other half, of course, is making sure they can afford to do something about it.

Although it works best in business-to-consumer environments, this approach can be harnessed effectively by a wide variety of businesses. The key lies in the offer: it has to be perceived to be valuable enough to warrant submitting an entry.

MAKE FRIENDS WITH
AN EDITOR

News happens fast, and when the media need information to help put together a story, they usually have little time to interview potential subject experts. That's why it makes sense to build relationships with media editors covering your area of expertise.

Start by identifying the editors that cover areas related to your business. With most publications, editors are assigned to specific coverage areas, known as "beats." You can usually get a full list of editors and their beats from the publication's web site. If they are not listed on the Internet, just call the main office number; beat assignment information is no secret, and is freely shared.

Once you have identified the appropriate editors, start a file to keep samples of some of their writing. This will help you get to know each editor's particular writing style and approach to news coverage.

To stay top of mind when the need for an expert arises, send a media kit containing the following:

- backgrounder on your business

- personal biography detailing your areas of expertise, and explaining why you are qualified to answer questions in the area of your expertise

- two or three recent articles and press releases that exemplify your knowledge of the subject

- Rolodex-style cards in two formats: one with your area of expertise as the header, followed by your name and contact information, and the other in the "standard" business card format of your name or the name of your company first, followed by the rest of your contact information.

After sending your package to an editor, call to introduce yourself and make sure they received your materials. Ask what sort of articles they are currently working on, and offer any information you can that might be of help.

Send Out Press Releases

The venerable press release is a staple item in an effective business promotion kit. Despite its history, however, companies often fail to use the press release to their best advantage. Consequently, they miss opportunities for exposure.

A press release is a story sent to the media for possible use. The goal is to catch media attention and get part or all of the release to appear in a publication, or on the TV or radio. Unlike advertising, which carries an inherent bias, media references, commentaries and articles have much higher credibility. Press releases can trigger all sorts of publicity, ranging from modest references to in-depth articles about your company, products and services.

An effective press release has three basic parts: contact information, the headline, and the body copy. Identify your company and put contact information where it can't be missed. It is essential that editors and program directors know how to reach you quickly.

The headline should briefly explain what the release is about. Its sole purpose is to get the attention of the editors to whom it is sent, and cause them to read the release. Keep it short, but make it potent!

The line or two that often appears just below the headline is the sub-head. Although not essential, you can use it to provide the "next level" of detail about the content.

The release should be less than two pages long. Start the first paragraph with Kipling's "Six Serving Men"—answer *Who What, When, Where, Why* and *How*—and tell the story as quickly as possible. Anything you write after that is supporting detail.

Perhaps the most important aspect of the release is not the release itself, however. Where most press releases fail is that they are not sent to the right media contacts. As a result, adequate exposure is virtually impossible. Keep an up-to-date media list handy at all times. This way, you will be able to move quickly and reach the right people when the time comes that you have a story to tell.

GIVE A BOOK REVIEW

From a book-buyer's perspective, one of the best parts of leading online bookseller Amazon.com is the many customer reviews that accompany most book listings. An invaluable supplement to the authors' own descriptions of their works, these third-party critiques add insights from others who have read the books, and often help buyers decide if the book will be of interest to them.

They also provide an opportunity for the reviewer to get a little bit of exposure. For example, at the time this Handbook was written, the following bio appeared as a book review for the book "Influence: *The Science of Persuasion*" by Dr. Robert Cialdini:

"Name: Michael Netzley
Reviewer Rank: 7906
About me: Michael is an independent communication consultant and management communication faculty member living in Asia and Europe. He currently serves as the President of GoldPoint Strategies, Inc. GoldPoint offers its clients an international perspective on communication strategy issues.

Michael also serves on the faculty of Singapore Management University, the Helsinki School of Economics (Finland) and the Bled School of Management (Slovenia). Michael specializes in communication strategy and persuasion…".

You get the idea.

Book reviews build your credibility in two ways. First, your own words give you an opportunity to illustrate your critical thinking ability. Second, you gain credibility through your association with a good author or book.

Although any book review will get you some exposure, it makes the most sense to focus on reviewing books that are relevant to your field, and likely to be of interest to your target market. You can get started writing reviews today, and write as little or as much as you like in each review.

Negotiate Reciprocal Link Exchanges

If you have a web site, a fundamental goal should be to get more visitors. Although you should promote your site offline as well as online, it is often far easier to get someone to your site if they are already sitting in front of their computer and browsing the Internet. If you can make it easy for people to click over to your site without having to type in your web site address, you're a step ahead of the game.

One way to do this is by developing a series of reciprocal links. Take a good look at other web sites frequented by your ideal prospect. In return for a link to your site, offer to provide one to theirs.

When other site owners create links to your site, they create opportunities for more visitors to find their way to your site. It's really that simple. The more links that exist, the more ways there are for visitors to find you. Think of your web site as you would a physical store. You wouldn't want to be the only business down a dead-end street, would you? Neither should you want to have only one way into your online store.

There are other reasons to seek out link exchanges. Some search engines—notably Google, the 800-pound gorilla—base their decisions about how high to rank sites on link popularity. In essence, the more links that exist to your site, the more likely it is to out-rank competitive sites that the search engines believe are not as popular.

Be judicious in your choice of partners, though. Just getting traffic isn't enough. The key is to get links from sites that are visited by the people you would most like to have visit your site. Ask prospective partners for the nitty-gritty details on who visits their site, how often, where they come from and whether or not they buy. Only then will you be informed enough to make the best decisions you can for your unique site and situation.

BUY PAY-PER-CLICK SEARCH ENGINE LISTINGS

Search Engines are the number one way that people find web sites. A shocking 41% of Internet users find sites this way. They are used much more often than simply guessing the URL (28%), word of mouth (13%), online advertising (10%), or print advertising (10%).

A key aspect that makes search engines a "killer app" for marketers is the fact that people only use them when they are looking for something. When someone searched for "Chicago museums," it is pretty clear what they are trying to find. There is no better way to reach people who have a direct and current interest in what you have to offer.

But simply being listed on an engine isn't enough. As searchers seldom scan down past the first page of listings, it pays to pay to be a *top-ranked* site.

Pay-per-click engines allow us to do just that. Simply put, pay-per-click let's us choose exactly how high we want to be in the search engines results listings.

The price we pay for the rank we want is determined by auction, and depends on how much competition there is for the keywords and phrases that are most relevant to our businesses. Whatever you do, make sure that you bid enough to be the first-second, or third-ranked site in Overture's pay-per-click search engine listing. If you are, your site will be carried over to a number of other search engines as well, dramatically increasing your exposure.

To get started with a pay-per-click campaign, take a look at Overture[1] (overture.com). They are the leading PPC engine, and an excellent place to get started. You will find clear instructions there about what to do first.

Here are a couple of web resources that every search engine marketer from the neophyte to the aficionado should know about: Danny Sullivan's Search Engine Watch (searchenginewatch.com), and Bruce Clay's site (bruceclay.com). They both provide plenty of information about all types of search engine strategies.

---

1. Now a Yahoo! company.

Sponsor Someone Else's Web Site or Portal

One of the keys to successful promotion is finding ways to get in front of prospective customers. With enough money, you can force your way in front of them. If you're like most businesses, however, it's not that easy. You've got a budget you've got to stick to, and it never quite seems to be enough.

Rather than trying to go to them, why not let prospects come to you? In other words, find out where your prospects go when they are looking for information related to what you have to offer, and be there! One way to do this is to sponsor a web site or portal.

A principal advantage of this approach is that you can take your time and review information about a site's visitors before you select which sites you sponsor. As a result you have complete control, and can literally choose the prospects you want to reach.

Start by determining exactly whom it is you want to reach. If you are a consumer-oriented company, how old are your typical prospects? Are they male or female? Are they married or single? If you sell other businesses, what sort of company is your best prospect? What is the typical title of the person who makes or exerts significant influence over the buying decision?

With this information in hand, put yourself in your prospects' shoes. Think about where they go when they are looking for information related to what you have to offer. If you sell supply chain management systems, for example, you may be able to sponsor the e-commerce portal on E-Commerce World (ecomworld.com). Many sites such as this allow companies to pay to sponsor e-mails, pages, or whole sections of the site. Doing so not only gets your message front and center before your prospect, it can also lend an air of credibility.

Launch An E-mail Campaign

The Internet has changed a lot of things. The most dramatic among them is how we communicate with each other. Although the Internet is used for research, gaming, and a wide variety of other purposes, the leading Internet activity for both personal and business users is sending and receiving e-mail.

Done right, e-mail marketing can be a highly effective way to get new business. Done poorly, you can quickly alienate an existing customer base, discourage new prospects from ever calling you, or even end up in very expensive lawsuit!

Like any direct marketing approach, e-mail marketing depends upon three fundamental components: the list of recipients, the promotional text (known as "copy"), and the offer. Of these, the most important aspect by far is the list. A bad offer to a good list will always draw more response than a good offer to a bad list.

A mailing list that you compile for your own business's use is referred to as a "house" list. Because the names on your house list are familiar with your business, house lists are more likely to contain good prospects than rented lists.

One issue of e-mail marketing that you must address is SPAM. In the pyramid of permission marketing, the pinnacle is double opt-in. This is the level to which all professional marketers should strive.

Building a house list through double opt-in permission e-mail marketing consists of the following steps:

- Potential respondents are offered an opportunity to join your list, and voluntarily elect to join (*opt-in*)

- Respondents receive an e-mail confirmation stating that they or someone else have requested that they be added to the mailing list (*confirmed opt-in*)

- The confirmation e-mail also asked respondents to reply to the e-mail to confirm their intent to join the list (*double opt-in*)

CREATE AN AUDIO PROGRAM

If you can speak for an hour about a topic related to your business, then you can create an audio program.

Putting your words on tape can help build your business in a number of ways. First of all, it provides a low-cost way to promote your business to potential customers. Once the program is recorded, it costs very little to make additional copies of the tape. Many businesses use tapes as a bait piece to get prospects to identify themselves. It stands to reason that anyone who requests your tape has an interest in its subject.

Another benefit of developing audio programs is that they are an easy cross-sell to customers who have just purchased other products or services. For example, someone who enjoys your seminar might easily pay an additional sum to buy an audio tape that discusses additional points on a subject of importance to them.

The first step in creating an audio presentation is to decide for whom you will create it. Audience selection is of paramount importance, for it influences everything from topic selection to program length to the creative approach employed. After you have chosen the audience, you must select a topic that is of sufficient interest to that market.

Once you've selected your audience and nailed down an appropriate topic, create a program outline. An outline is essential to keep you on track and within the time you have selected for your program length. Without one, it is far too easy to start into a rambling, directionless monologue that fails to deliver the impact you intend.

Don't rule this avenue out just because you don't think you have the voice to make an audio program. There are plenty of resources around to help produce a quality tape. And it makes no difference that the voice your prospects hear isn't your own. What matters is that they get to know a little bit about you, you establish credibility, and they think of you when they have a need for the services you provide.

Change the Channel

Though it may seem counter-intuitive to the uninitiated, a strong customer relationship is often much more important than a good product or a low price. If you don't have the relationship yourself, you may be able to "buy" it using channels.

Effective use of channels—distributors and resellers of your products or services—can open the door to sales that would be impossible to reach on your own.

There are three generic points on the distribution continuum: intensive, selective, and exclusive. Generally, intensive distribution is for commodity products, selective distribution is used where there is moderate differentiation between competing brands, and exclusive distribution is used for specialty goods, where a high-quality image is supported by limited product availability.

Select channel members carefully. Remember that your ultimate customer often sees your partners as an extension of your business. A manufacturer or service provider that prides itself on providing products or services of the highest quality must be very careful about the kinds of channel members that it chooses to sell its offerings. If its products were to be represented by low-status channel members, there could be long-term consequences for its reputation. A rose by any other name may smell as sweet, but how good could a Porsche be, if it was bought off a Chevy lot?

In evaluating potential channel members, consider candidates' credit and financial condition, sales strength, product lines, reputation, market coverage, sales performance, management succession, management ability, attitude and size.

Your channel strategy must be compatible with your product, price, and promotional plans. And these must be compatible with your overall goals and objectives. Achieving this kind of balance is what professional business management is all about, and also what makes resounding success such an elusive target.

SET UP A WEB SITE

The Internet's role in promoting and enabling commercial activity is undeniable. And it's power grows with each passing day. For example, Internet use has recently surpassed TV as the media with the greatest number of hours used per week, for the average person.

Especially if you're trying to reach a younger audience, there are few media better to make sure that you hit your mark. Statistics released in early 2004 show that 8.8% of girls and 12.2% of boys aged eight to 12 years old have their own web sites. Even more remarkably, according to a BRANDchild study, 22 percent of tweens (kids eight to 14) have already purchased online!

Without question, the Internet will play an even more important role in commerce as these kids grow into income-earning consumers with a full range of interests and responsibilities. Whether your business sells to consumers or other businesses, you can't afford to ignore the Internet.

There are five basic steps you must take as you put your web site together:

1. Develop a Site Strategy

- *Figure out who you're trying to attract*
- *Script out the steps you want prospects to take*
- *Plan how to move prospects through these steps*

2. Prepare Your Web Site

- *Choose and register your domain name*
- *Set up a visitor tracking system*

3. Use Search Engines and Directories

- *Do keyword research*
- *Optimize your web site*
- *Submit your site to the major engines*
- *Deploy a pay-per-click campaign*

4. Build 1-to-1 Customer Relationships

- *Drive traffic to your site*
- *Show off your products or expertise*
- *Get permission to contact them by e-mail*
- *Promote to them regularly*

5. Continuously Test Various Traffic-Drivers

Write A Book

Few things can enhance your credibility more effectively than authoring a book. Authors are frequently perceived as subject matter experts in their fields. This notoriety leads to a range of opportunities to generate leads and close new business. Most books provide only modest revenues, but they can help launch a speaking career and get you in front of audiences ripe for your message.

For most people with something to write about, the only thing standing between them and writing a book is time. The best way to get started is simply that: get started. Set aside a few minutes each week for writing. Thirty minutes, an hour, a morning each week. As much time as you can afford. The key is that you start today, and make every effort to keep the writing dates you set with yourself.

Perhaps you want to write, but you really don't think that your writing is up to snuff. You can always have a book written for you. This is known as ghost-writing, and it is more common than many people realize. With your guidance, a competent ghost writer can research and write a book in your subject area in a relatively short period of time.

Prices and terms can usually be negotiated. Most ghost writers will quote a flat fee for their work. You set the prices and keep any monies from selling the book.

Although it can take months or years to find a publisher who will work with you, you can always go the self-publishing route. This means that you will not automatically end up on the shelves of your local bookstores, and you will have to manage the distribution of the book yourself.

You do not have to print hundreds or thousands of copies of your book at one time. Some printers will print your book on demand, one copy at a time. An example is Café Press (cafepress.com/cp/info/sell/books.aspx). For just four-and-a-half cents per page for printing plus a $4 binding fee, you can get your work printed and saddle-stitched. This means that a 150-page book will cost $10.75 to produce. What you charge your customers over and above that price is completely up to you.

Publish A Newspaper

If you've got something to say, and need to keep in touch with prospects over a long period of time, a great way to maintain a following is to publish a newspaper.

One of the most successful organizations to use newspapers for lead generation comes, predictably, from the field of advertising copy writing. The outstanding exemplar is The Wizard of Ads (wizardofads.com). Their free publication, *The Beagle Bugle,* is published on a monthly basis, and distributed to a very large audience.

If a single article can influence opinion and build your reputation, then a newspaper is credibility on steroids! It's hard not to take a business seriously, when they go to the effort of producing a full-sized, broadsheet newspaper on authentic newsprint. That's a style that screams, "Trust us—we know *exactly* what we're doing!"

The key to publishing a paper that becomes more than an exercise in grammar and spelling is content. You have to maintain reader interest, so you must be able to write or otherwise collect enough newsworthy content on a regular basis, or your readers will tune out by the second issue.

Don't worry if you don't have the time, equipment or experience to format a newspaper. Any printer can recommend a number of layout and design agencies, and many can provide this service for you themselves.

Another option is to hire a student from a local graphic arts program who is interested in doing this type of work. If you follow this path, just make sure that you have their commitment to continue for a defined period of time, no matter what. Also, plan ahead of time to find a suitable replacement, when their contract is coming to an end. Continuity is very important, and even subtle changes in design styles can have a surprising affect on audience loyalty.

Exhibit At Trade Shows

Virtually every industry—from contact lens manufacturing to customer relationship management software to comic book retailing—has its own trade shows. And for good reason, too: there are no more effective forums for meeting a large number of prospective customers in one place. These events can be massive, often attracting tens of thousands of visitors, and hundreds of exhibitors.

If you go, the key is to be prepared. Prepare your booth, prepare your materials, prepare your scripts and, most importantly, prepare your people. Have clear goals for what you want to accomplish, and a carefully devised plan for what to say to those who visit your booth.

One of the main reasons that many companies fail to come away from trade shows with a suitable amount of *qualified* leads to pursue is that they have not spent the time required to train their staff effectively. They simply fill the floor with sales reps and hope for the best. Make sure that your booth staff follow these guidelines:

Resolve to speak with everyone—studies show that just one in every 20 trade show visitors is a hot prospect. Follow the "Engage, Qualify, and Eliminate" rule. Make as many contacts as possible, determine if they are or are not potential buyers, quickly but politely ditch the tire kickers, and plan to follow through with serious prospects after the show.

Sell only benefits from the word "Go"—the average trade show conversation lasts less than five minutes, so don't waste time talking about features. Get right to the heart of the matter, and tell visitors clearly and succinctly how your products or services will benefit them.

Send A Sales Letter

Do you ever wonder why a greater number of sales letters continue to arrive in your business and personal mail, year after year after year? Because they work, that's why!

Although many of the sales letters we receive are poor examples of the craft, the truth is that more letters than we might imagine do meet their objectives.

One of the chief benefits of sales letters is their *targetability*. Because you send the letters, you can choose exactly who to send them to. In addition, you can send them in the quantities and at the frequency that suit your budget, and your desire for leads.

By now, you probably have the format down cold: outer envelope with "teaser" copy, multi-page sales letter, promotional brochure, and inner "return" envelope.

Like any direct marketing technique, the three keys to success are test, test, and test! Don't expect a sales letter to achieve perfection without making any changes. If that's your approach, you'll never know for sure whether your mailer is the best that it can be! Instead, send several copies of your letter, and then change it up a bit and send it again. Measure the response rates from each version, and adopt the changes that achieve a higher response. It won't take many iterations to find out what works and what doesn't.

Common elements of a sales letter to test include:

- The Mailing List
- The Size of the Envelope
- The Envelope Copy
- The Offer
- The Length of the Body Copy

Aside from the mailer itself, the two other critical components of a successful mailing are the mailing list and the offer. In fact, some direct mail experts point to the *40/40/20 Rule of Direct Mailing*. Specifically, 40% of your success depends on your mailing list, 40% on your offer, and only 20% on the mailer itself.

Participate In E-Zines, Forums & Newsgroups

If you're like most people that have used the Internet, you've belonged to at least one Internet forum, newsgroup or e-mail list, at one time or another. It's only natural: people need a sense of community in their lives, and instinctively seek to fill that need by congregating—online and offline—with others who have similar interests.

Publishing or overseeing your own online e-zine, forum or newsgroup is a fool-proof way to gain direct access to the precise audience you seek. If getting into publishing isn't for you, at least make it a habit to seek out and actively participate in online forums run by others where your target audience congregates. Offering your knowledge and advice through such forums is one way to build credibility quickly, and can position you as an expert in your field with very little effort.

There are a couple of things to keep in mind if you would like to start using forums and newsgroups for business promotion. Before posting anything yourself, spend some time reading what others have posted, and get a sense of the flavor of the discussion. This is commonly referred to as "lurking," and is essential etiquette in any online public forum.

Every group is different, and the nature of the discussions will vary widely from forum to forum. When you finally get an opportunity to post something yourself, it is important that your post be relevant, and perceived as that of an insider. Remember that a key aspect of any business communications tactic is credibility. Also, go out of your way to avoid bias, and never post any overt commercial messages. Doing so is the surest way to get "flamed" by another forum member. This refers to the searing messages often sent when a message poster abuses the privilege of membership, and blatantly posts a message consisting of little more than self-centered promotion.

HOLD AN OPEN HOUSE

Even if yours is not the type of business where customers typically come to see you at your location, you can benefit from holding an open house. Open houses are a great way to generate new leads, as well to get "on the fence" prospects to budge.

Promote your open house as a way to come out and meet the team. Your invitation should sell the opportunity for guests to become acquainted with your staff and to learn a few things about how you do what you do.

Keep your event to less than four hours, and remember that the best time for an open house is from 10:00 a.m. to 2:00 p.m. By incorporating the lunch hour, you increase your chances of getting more people because they can fit in a stop to your location during their normal lunch break.

Once you've pulled off a successful event the first time, you might even consider making your open house an annual event. You can hold open houses more frequently, although the novelty will wear off quickly if you try it any more often than once or twice a year.

Wear nametags. Make it easy for guests to get to know you and your staff.

Give a demonstration. Show off a new product, or teach customers how you do some of the things you do.

Give something away. Everyone should receive something they can show off to coworkers who didn't attend. Even small items go a long way. Alternatively, hold a drawing and give away a grand prize and a few consolation prizes. This gives you a convenient way to build a mailing list of those interested in what you offer.

Put out a suggestion box. Ask visitors to the open house to provide any suggestions they have for improving the quality of your products or services.

Start A Newsletter

If you have a large pool of prospects and you're looking for a way to keep in touch cost-effectively, consider publishing a regular newsletter. Newsletter publishing is one of the best ways to keep a pool of prospects "warm" until they are ready to buy from you.

An e-zine (pronounced "Ee-zeen", like "magazine") is simply an electronic newsletter, published via e-mail or over the Internet. Not only are publishing costs much lower, but there are no unread copies to go in the trash. As well, since e-zines are distributed as soon as you hit the [send] key, you can work to tighter deadlines. Paper newsletters can require a significant lead time for printing.

Like other forms of publishing, one of the chief benefits of newsletters is credibility. Very few things can position you as an expert faster than getting your words in print.

If what you write (which is referred to as "content") is interesting and useful, you will keep your subscribers' interest and they look forward to reading the next issue.

It's easy to get started publishing a newsletter or e-zine. All you need is a theme and a list of the names of potential subscribers. Create a schedule of topics that fit with your chosen theme, and start to plan out what you will write about on each planned publishing date.

Don't despair if you can't write well enough yourself to create your own newsletter articles. The content you publish does not have to be your own. It simply has to be of interest and value to your target audience.

If you can't talk qualified colleagues, friends or neighbors into writing for you, there are plenty of article syndication sites on the Internet where you can pick up articles at little or no cost. Just keep in mind as you sort through the available articles that some of the authors may be your direct competitors. Of course you'll want to take a pass on these, and look for authors who represent less of a competitive threat to your business.

SET UP A CROSS-PROMOTION

Cross-promotions are a great way to extend your lead generation initiative into local neighborhoods. The advantages of cross promotions come down to the "Three C's": *Cost, Control, and Credibility.*

Cost—Cross promotions cost much less than many other promotional activities because distribution of your offer is done through a third party instead of traditional media.

Control—Cross promotions offer several types of control. First of all, because you decide the number of promotional pieces distributed, you control how many people can redeem your offer. This lets you set a limit on your financial exposure. Secondly, by selecting which businesses you will cross promote with, you have control over the geographic area in which your offer is distributed. This lets you avoid providing discounts and incentives to people who already buy from you.

Credibility—If you discount your own products or services frequently, your customers will come to expect a discount every time they buy from you. When the added value is provided courtesy of someone else, your customers will attribute the advantage to the third party, and not automatically look to you to reduce your prices or provide extra benefits.

There are many ways to set up cross-promotions, but here are a few ideas you might try to get started.

- Offer a discount from regular retail pricing if customers buy from both you and your partner.

- Give out samples of each others' products.

- Pool prospect lists and send out joint mailings.

- Mention how your partners' products can be used with yours.

In order for the partnership to succeed, there must be some similarity in the markets you and your partners serve, and your products must be complementary goods or services that do not compete with each other.

Use Community
Bulletin Boards

Depending on the type of customers you are trying to reach, you might want to consider using the network of bulletin boards spread out across your community. There are boards in literally hundreds of locations in every community. What's more, as messages can be posted on many bulletin boards for free, this can be one of the most cost-effective ways to reach a large number of people.

Before you discard bulletin boards with a huff, and say, "these are not for me," think about who you are trying to reach, and what you are trying achieve. While it is true that this approach is not for everyone, many businesses find this a terrific way to target certain customer segments. Real estate agents use boards to reach apartment-dwellers thinking of buying their first home. Delivery services use message boards to reach seniors who have difficulty getting home from grocery stores after shopping. And alarm-monitoring companies leave messages about the risks of not protecting your home against intrusion.

Another advantage of using this method is that you have complete control over the geographic territory in which your messages appear. You can determine how many and which sorts of neighborhoods should be exposed to your messages. In addition, you can choose exactly when your message should appear, and when it should be removed. This is terrific for businesses promoting date-specific events or limited-time offers.

There are a huge number of bulletin boards in a wide variety of settings in every community. You can find them in many apartment complexes, grocery stores, coffee shops, waiting rooms, schools, churches, hospitals, and government offices. You might need permission to post a message on some boards, and some might automatically remove postings after certain periods to ensure that others have an opportunity to use the space, too.

SEND POSTCARDS

It's true. Postcards aren't just for vacationers any more!

In a trend that started in the real estate industry, all sorts of businesses are turning to postcards as a fast and cost-effective way to get their messages out.

Because they do not have to be opened, cards break through the clutter more easily than other direct mail. For the same reason, they represent less *risk* to the recipient, who can quickly scan the offer and make a decision about what to do next, without having to open and read a letter.

There is another significant advantage to using postcards instead of other mail pieces. The United States Postal Service charges only $0.23 to deliver a postcard anywhere in country, which is about 38% cheaper than the cost of mailing a standard-sized letter.

Typical postcards measure 4–1/4" by 6," but a wide variety of other formats are available, too.

Cards can be printed very economically, even in smaller quantities. It is not hard to find a printer that can produce 1,000 full color cards, printed on both sides, for less than $150. And as many as 10,000 cards can be had for $390!

There are a couple of other variations on the postcard theme. Some entrepreneurs and clever salespeople buy everyday postcards off the shelf, and send hand-written notes to their prospects and best customers. The results are usually positive, as recipients are impressed that the sender took the time to write and send a personal card.

Another option is to design and print cards that you give away to your customers to send to *their own* family, friends or prospects. The cards need to be attractive, and be something that your customers would want to send. Of course, they also carry your company name and logo, and a brief message. Cards such as these can enhance your credibility in much the same way as a personal referral from the sender.

Ask Your Friends

After customers, the people who know your business and its products, services and capabilities best are usually your friends and family. And yet, most people don't take the opportunity to ask their close associates for referrals to potential new clients.

For some, perhaps, it's a matter of pride. They prefer not to do anything that makes it look like they need more business. Well, get over it! This is business, after all, and not asking may mean the difference between modest and outstanding success.

The simple truth is that your existing circle of friends may be all you need to find a way to get to the clients you've been trying so hard to reach. There is a lot to be said for the *"Six Degrees of Separation"* principle. For example, if you know only 200 people, and each of those people knew 200 more people, your personal network after just one "level" is now 40,000 people! That's 40,000 contacts that you can get to, just by making it clear to your friends and family what kind of contact you are looking to make.

The key to connecting through your friends and family is how you explain what it is that you do or offer. Take some time to develop a personal "audio ad" for yourself. An audio ad is a 5-to 10-second sound bite that describes your business in such a way that people understand and can easily remember the value you have to provide. Be clear, but be brief. If the audio ad is hard to remember, it won't be repeated. And an audio ad that doesn't get repeated does you no good whatsoever.

If asking friends for a personal introduction isn't for you, there are alternatives. An Internet-based service called Linked-In (linkedin.com) connects people with others for the purpose of making business connections, finding employees and contractors, finding company contacts or industry experts, or connecting people interested in new projects or job leads. For the time being, Linked-In is a free service. A note on the company web site states that this may change when the system completes beta-testing, however.

Not surprisingly, Linked-In's outstanding popularity has drawn competitors including Ryze (ryze.com) and Orkut (orkut.com). Check into one or all of these and watch your network grow.

Join A Service Club

Service Clubs are member organizations that have been formed so that their members may volunteer to perform valuable community services, enjoy fellowship, learn from knowledgeable speakers, develop and exercise leadership skills, expand business through professional networking, and participate in activities that provide a sense of real accomplishment.

Like many other forms of networking, membership in a service club can quickly put you in touch with a large number of people. The contacts you make by joining a service club include other club members, as well as the groups your service club exists to serve.

Business networking through service clubs is usually very low-key. This means that, while it might take longer than you would like to identify prospects and initiate business discussions with them, the personal relationships tend to be stronger. And strong personal relationships generally lead to better business relationships.

There are a large number of service clubs out there, and each has its own focus and mandate. You may wish to check out some of the following:

- Altrusa
- Civitan Club
- Exchange
- Kinsman Club
- Kiwanis Club
- Lions Club
- Rotary Club
- Zonta International

Most clubs will permit you to attend a couple of meetings without charge, so that you can decide if a particular club is for you. If you agree with a club's mandate but attend a meeting and don't find it to your taste, try visiting another chapter of the same service club. Each chapter has a definite "personality" and, just because you don't click with the first group doesn't mean that club is not for you.

VOLUNTEER

Aside from furthering the mandate of whatever volunteer organizations you join, offering some of your time for free can be a very sound way to build relationships, generate leads and get more business for your business.

Boards of directors, organizing committees, and ad hoc work groups can all put you in contact with people you might not otherwise have a way to meet.

Perhaps the most well known of all volunteer organizations is the United Way (national.unitedway.org). With a history dating back to 1918 the United Way has built its reputation on "bringing communities together to focus on the most important needs in the community—building partnerships, forging consensus and leveraging resources to make a measurable difference".

Another excellent place to volunteer is the YMCA (ymca.net). Most every city or town in the United States is home to least one branch of this popular organization. In metropolitan areas, it is common for there to be a central "metro" board as well as a separate governing board for each YMCA branch. Depending on the type of person you are trying to reach, both levels can be good places to meet new contacts.

Habitat for Humanity (habitat.org) is an example of an organization where volunteers come together as ad hoc groups to work on a project. Commitments tend to be short—sometimes as short as a single day—so you must plan to move quickly and use time well if you are thinking of prospecting through this agency.

The key to making volunteering pay off as a business development activity is finding out what kind of people you will be volunteering with. Who sits on the board you are thinking of joining? What sort of person helps organize a walk-a-thon? Would the people who volunteer on that fundraising committee be good prospects for you? Find out, and then pitch in! But remember to keep your approaches low-key, or you risk turning off your prospect and ruining any chance you have of doing any business.

Teach a College Course

A great way to get exposure in your community is to teach a college course on a subject related to your business. Some people enjoy teaching within the hallowed halls of four-year colleges. Others prefer the practical environments of community colleges or technical schools. Both offer opportunities for business development, albeit in different ways.

Four-year programs are typically filled with eager young students, most often working on their first degrees. The opportunity here is not usually found in the classroom itself. Rather, the payoff comes from developing the reputation as an expert in your field.

In contrast, community college and technical school classes tend to have a greater proportion of adult learners. As a result, the chance is much greater that you will meet someone who has a clear and present need for your services, or who is in a position to influence someone who does.

If you are a confident and well-organized presenter, teaching people who might be in a position to buy from you has a remarkable effect on business development. You establish instant credibility, and position yourself as an expert in the field.

To get a teaching assignment, start by calling the universities and community colleges in your local area. Although there may be other avenues in some institutions, a good place to start is the Continuing Education department. Continuing Education training is more likely to be delivered during evenings and weekends, and will likely be easier to fit in to your already-busy schedule. There is also a much greater likelihood that your class will be filled with adult learners, who are better prospects for most businesses than college-aged students.

You may also want to check the faculty openings sections of schools in your area. Positions do open up, from time to time, and some need to be filled on very short notice.

Hand Out Your Card

How many times has a business card convinced you to do something? In all likelihood, not very often if ever at all. The reason for this is that most business cards are boring and ineffective.

But it doesn't have to be that way. Your business cards can be virtual viral selling machines that work on their own to help generate leads.

Here are a few ideas:

Prize, contest or giveaway business cards. Print a serial number on the back of each of your cards. Offer a weekly prize on your website, and let everyone who receives your card know about it so that they will visit your website periodically to see if they have won.

Irresistible benefit and/or bounce back business cards. Use your cards as a coupon promoting some irresistible benefit for your prospects that will get them to come back to you. For example, you might offer prospects the chance to redeem your card for a free upgrade, lesson, sample, or discount of some type.

Viral marketing business cards. Include some sort of incentive so that your business cards are not only redeemed, but also passed around. For instance, you might have a place on your cards where the person who is passing out your cards can write their name. You can offer them an additional bonus, discount or gift for every card that is redeemed that has their name on it. Most people would be happy to pass out your business cards if they received something that they consider valuable in return for their efforts.

Give A Seminar

If teaching a full-semester college class isn't for you, there is yet another way to get exposure on the local speaking scene. Give a seminar.

Long a staple activity of professional services firms, seminars are a great way to build credibility and generate leads for your enterprise. They give you a chance to show off your knowledge and professionalism, and provide a great opportunity for attracting and qualifying prospects.

There are several ways to get started in seminars. The easiest way to edge into this high-contact lead generation activity is to get someone to sponsor you. Chambers of Commerce, Ad & Sales Clubs, and a variety of other community organizations seek out seminar leaders to present to their membership. You might also try contacting some of the following potential seminar sponsors, who frequently hire facilitators for in-house workshops:

- Professional Networking Groups
- City Departments and Public Agencies

- Managers of Mid-sized and Large Corporations
- Industry Association Meeting Planners

Trade show organizers contract with a large number of speakers to manage their breakout sessions. Although the lead-time for getting involved may be several months in advance of the event, presenting at these events can be a great way to connect with your target audiences.

Once you've got the hang of it, the next step is to organize and hold your own public seminar. Once you've developed good content, this isn't as daunting as it may seem. Hotels and other meeting spaces are accustomed to working with seminar providers, and can help you coordinate all of the physical logistics. Market your seminar using a combination of your own prospect list and e-mail or newsletter sponsorships for other relevant businesses. "Piggybacking" on others' mailings can help build credibility, and often gets good results.

Join The Chamber Of Commerce

Nearly every city or town has its own Chamber of Commerce. These groups are not-for-profit organizations set up by local business leaders to promote business growth, provide personal and professional development opportunities, and affect local public policy decisions.

Some Chambers flourish and provide many events throughout the year. Others are less active, counting monthly member meetings among their only regularly scheduled activities. In any event, the majority are worth joining if one of your goals is to generate new business.

Chamber membership can be effective for any company, but those serving small and mid-sized businesses have found membership especially rewarding. Sooner or later, most new companies join the Chamber. This is what makes the Chamber the place to be.

But there's a catch. It's not enough just to *join* the Chamber. That's like buying an exercise bike and expecting to lose weight without riding it. You have to actively *use* your membership, in order to turn up leads.

Take advantage of the many programs your Chamber offers. Go to the new member orientation. Sign up for management and personal development classes. Attend the luncheons and picnics. *See, and be seen!*

If you find the Chamber to be a good source of prospects for your business, volunteer for a leadership position with the Chamber. As with volunteer positions with service clubs and not-for-profit agencies, there's no better way to help people get to know you than to meet with them regularly, and lead them in some activity.

You don't have to be a board member, either. There are plenty of other volunteer opportunities available, and most offer the chance to work closely with others. Membership coordination, event planning, and member communications are all worthwhile volunteer positions to seek out and hold.

WRITE ARTICLES

A tried and true way to evidence your expertise and get exposure for your business is to write articles. This is done in every industry and, if you can put a few lines together on a subject worth reading about, there are a wide variety of publications that will distribute your work.

Some publications will pay for articles, while others will give only credit and a brief contributor's bio in return for your work. Even for those that pay, don't expect your writing to create a new profit center for your company; the pay is meager. For example, at the time of this writing, the principal daily newspaper of one mid-sized U.S. metropolitan market pays a flat $50 for 900-word articles on business topics.

Most daily newspapers will consider running articles written by non-staff. Although details vary from publication to publication, a general guide is to aim for 800 to 1,000 words. This may sound like quite a bit, if you don't write much. But once you get the hang of it, you will soon find that it is often difficult to keep your words about a popular topic down in that range.

Another option for distributing your printed work is to distribute it through a few of the online article distribution sites. Sites such as ideamarketers.com can get your material out to a large audience very quickly.

Even more powerful than being posted on these sites themselves, however, is the opportunity for secondary distribution in other publications. Once your article is posted, don't be surprised to find your work appearing in newsletters, e-zines, and on web sites for companies of which you've never heard. Those using your articles are supposed to ask permission from the author first, and most usually do. Most authors are happy to grant permission provided that they get credit for the article at the end of the article, in a space commonly referred to as a "resource box". Secondary distribution such as this can drive up your web site traffic and encourage offline inquiries by people with an interest in what you offer.

Sponsor A Mailing

Many not-for-profit organizations send regular mailings to their membership and patrons. If their target audiences match the profiles of your ideal prospects, there may be an opportunity for you to reach your prospects while simultaneously providing a valuable service to the non-profit agency.

Cost control is critically important to non-profits, so they constantly look for ways to eliminate or reduce their expenses. For organizations with large member or donor bases, one expense area that can stand to be reduced is postage costs.

In some cases, non-profit agencies allow third-party sponsorship of their mailings. In return for paying postage costs, sponsors get the opportunity to distribute their own marketing message to the agency's members. Considering the credibility that can be gained from being associated with certain not-for-profit organizations, this can be a terrific promotional venue.

Call the Executive Directors of organizations whose members you wish to target and ask if they mail information to their constituents. If they do, explain your interest and set an appointment to meet with them to discuss your idea. Don't be too aggressive if they are not receptive to your proposal. If they're not willing to speak with you about sponsoring a mailing, it's not worth forcing the issue. Thank them for speaking with you and move on to the next agency.

When you do find a group that is willing to talk about working with you in this way, find out how many pieces they mail and how often they mail them. Then calculate the postage costs and the cost of producing your own information piece to include in the mailing.

As an added bonus, there may also be an additional financial incentive for helping non-profit organizations in this way. Ask the organization if a portion of your contribution can be considered a donation, which would qualify you for an income tax credit.

GIVE THEM SANDWICHES

Take a stroll down practically any street in central Brussels between the hours of four p.m. and midnight, and you're bound to be asked more than once or twice to step inside one of the city's many restaurants for a meal. Well-groomed pitchmen with irresistible charm call out to pass-ers-by and describe the fare with poetic perfection. For Belgian restau-ranteurs, it's a simple matter of survival. There are just too many good restaurants vying for patrons to leave it to chance that you'll choose to dine with them.

Can we take a lesson from that? If our businesses are in highly competi-tive industries, of course we can! And some in the U.S. already have. A few restaurants in cities including Charleston, South Carolina and San Francisco, California already employ this tactic. But it's an approach that does not have to be limited to food establishments.

In fact, some businesses have used similar tactics for decades. Street vendors bearing sandwich boards have directed pedestrians to muse-ums, flower shops, car dealerships, dry cleaners, parking lots, and a wide variety of other things. Even the Church of Scientology uses of this sort of sidewalk intercept approach. They lure unsuspecting prospects with the offer of a free personality assessment they refer to the as "Oxford Standard Capacity Test".

The key benefits to this "man-on-the-street" approach to lead generation all stem from the concept of *control*. You control everything. Location, timing, who to approach. Everything is completely up to you.

To use this approach, start by figuring out what to do or say to catch people's attention. The Scientologists use the simple and straightforward, "Excuse me. Have you ever taken the Oxford Standard Capacity Test?" If passers by say they've never heard of the test and ask more about it, the interceptor rolls smoothly into a well-rehearsed spiel that builds curiosity and encourages prospects to step inside to take the free test.

In contrast, Belgian restauranteurs often push their chocolate or waffles. If you've ever had either, then I'm sure you recognize the stopping power of this suggestion. Yum!

Get Outside

When it comes to reaching people outdoors, there is a nearly limitless supply of options. Billboards, bus boards, transit benches & shelters, backboards in ball parks and arenas, marquees, banners, and more. Nearly everything that can carry an ad, does. We're even confronted with outdoor ads in public restrooms!

Another creative outdoor medium that has popped up in recent years is "Wild Posting". This is the term used when dozens or hundreds of identical posters are plastered up side-by-side along building walls and on the wooden hoardings around construction sites in urban areas. Although it started out as promotional option of necessity for impoverished bands just starting out, Wild Posting is now an accepted practice used by some of the world's major consumer goods manufacturers.

Outdoor advertising provides three main advantages. The first is attention-getting power. Unlike newspaper, television or radio ads, outdoor ads don't have to vie for your attention and break through the clutter of competing ads, news or editorial content. Outdoor media options are usually placed so that members of their target audiences are exposed to them when their ability to concentrate and absorb their messages is at a peak.

A second advantage is affordability. On a CPM (cost per thousand people exposed) basis, it's tough to beat outdoor. Outdoor media reach large audiences at reasonable costs.

Finally, outdoor media offer the ability to pinpoint a geographic location. If you are opening a new store or trying to take the wind out a competitor's grand opening, for example, you can zero in on a neighborhood and make an impact with outdoor media.

If you're just getting started with outdoor media, begin by working with a small local ad agency. They usually know their service areas well. They can help design creative that will get your message across effectively, select the best options for your particular campaign, and negotiate rates on your behalf.

Tell 'em Where To Go With Signs

Come Friday afternoon, it seems that nearly every inch of every street corner in suburban America holds a sign of some sort. *Sign, sign, everywhere a sign.* Signs advertise real estate for sale, open houses, restaurants, schools, hair salons, gym memberships, babysitting and lawn care services, and any number of home-based business opportunities.

Municipal ordinances keep many signs away Monday to Friday, but a weekend exception or lax enforcement seems to open the door for these signs after city enforcement officers have put away their badges and ticket books for the week.

There are several reasons why signs can work well, for some businesses. To a certain extent, you reach a captive audience. There's often little for motorists to do when they reach a red light than look at the signs alongside their cars, while they wait for their turn to proceed. It's also very easy to target a market by location. If you want more traffic from a certain neighborhood, put out your signs over there. If you want to avoid promoting to a certain region, don't put any signs out.

Signs are also cheap to produce and distribute. Even if some get stolen through the weekend it's not likely to break your bank account to have to replace a few, each month.

The first step in using signs to promote your enterprise should be to call city hall and inquire about the relevant regulation. Just because businesses put out signs on the corner near your house doesn't mean that it's legal to do so. There can be fines involved and, while some established businesses can count fines as a cost of doing business, your business may not have that financial luxury.

Once you know the rules, call the city engineering department and ask for Annual Average Daily Traffic (AADT) data. These figures show the traffic volume for every street in your city, and can help you decide where your signs would be most effective.

Lastly, visit your local sign company to take a look at your options. There are all make and manner of signs available at a wide range of price points.

Go On Tour

Although the thought of touring might bring to mind images of aging British invasion rock and roll bands, the truth is that cross-country tours are not just for musicians anymore.

Organizations of all sizes tour the country each year to strengthen relationships with existing customers and drum up new leads. Computer hardware manufacturer Hewlett-Packard, software Developer Red Hat, and the Republican Party are among those who use this technique successfully.

Imagine the impact of a vendor coming to visit, "just because." Not a sales call, not a service call. Just a chance to say "We appreciate you. Thanks for buying from us."

Touring can be cost-effective. Red Hat executives say that even though they flew around the world, the total investment was one-fifth the cost of exhibiting at a major tradeshow.

Here are some guidelines to consider if you think a tour might be just the ticket to connect with your biggest fans:

Think loyalty, not acquisition. Plan your tour itinerary to hit cities where you already have somewhat of a following.

Let 'em know you're coming. Give at least two months' notice. Send plenty of stories about previous tour stops to build word of mouth. Encourage customers to invite others.

Build a buzz. Create a website with a schedule, descriptions of events, and extremely easy sign up. Update a tour blog every day with commentary, photos, customer testimonials, and videos or sound files.

Be generous with souvenirs, wearables and gifts. Bring lots of free stuff. Everybody loves a present.

Leave the suits at home. Serve beer. Be slightly outrageous. Have fun. A tour is for customers, not your banker.

Connect with customers. Influential, connected customers love to meet the people behind businesses, and will happily tell colleagues and about their rock-star meeting with you.

BUY AND SELL ON EBAY

Albeit one of the more unusual ways to get people to your web site, eBay can be used effectively as an avenue for lead generation. The simplest way to do this is to plaster your web address in your auction listings.

The tremendous volume of users navigating the auction site on a daily basis makes it a valuable and cost-effective method of "getting in the way" of prospective customers for your enterprise. Even if what you're promoting has nothing to do with what you buy and sell at auction, you can easily gain valuable exposure for your site and siphon off some traffic you might not have been able to get otherwise. Of course, if what you buy and sell on eBay relates to your main business, that's all the better!

Some clever entrepreneurs have even found ways to use their web site domain name as their eBay Username. While eBay frowns on this practice, the company has stopped short of initiating repercussions on those who use this to their advantage.

If you want to give it a try, simply place an asterisk before and after your web address, and the eBay system will not be able to recognize it for what it is. For example, *youcantseeme.com* would be a perfectly legitimate eBay Username, as far as eBay's site is concerned. As you buy and sell on eBay, your Username silently promotes your web site for you. This can get your domain name seen by hundreds or thousands of people, depending on how often you use the site and the popularity of the items that you buy and sell.

If you've already got an eBay domain name, you can change it by logging in on eBay and changing it through the "Change Your User ID" option in the "services" section.

Another way to get some attention is to list your URL in the "location" field instead of entering your city and state, when you list an item for auction. You can put anything you like there so why not advertise your website? For that section you don't need to use asterisks.

Watch the News

Clipping and media monitoring services aren't new to the PR world. But how you use them can make all the difference. Most firms use them as a way to track news on their own company, or on their closest competitors. As it turns out, they're missing a significant opportunity.

Take an example from one clever entrepreneur in Rockford, Illinois. Rather than retaining a clipping service just to track his own firm in yesterday's news, he's found a way to use the service as a powerful weapon in his lead generation arsenal.

He chooses key words that relate to his clients' businesses, and that help him qualify prospective clients as candidates for his services. The clipping service scans the media and sends him e-mails of articles that contain his chosen key words. Using what he learns in those articles, he then hunts down the company's CEO and faxes over a personalized letter introducing his company and his services.

To help get the prospects on the hook, he offers a free consultation. This low-risk, direct approach fits perfectly with the high-priced professional services this entrepreneur offers, and response has been high. Sales have risen six-fold since he started using the clipping service.

The leaders in the media monitoring industry are Bacons (bacons.com) and Luce (burrellesluce.com). However, the field is growing quickly, and new entrants have brought about competitive pricing and terms.

If you decide to look into media clipping as a lead generation tactic, here are a few other online clipping and monitoring services you may want to check out:

- cyberalert.com
- clipgenius.com
- ewatch.com
- tveyes.com
- metrica.net
- traderlock.com

BLOG

Just when you thought you really knew the web…

> **Blog**: *(n.) Short for Web log, a blog is a Web page that serves as a publicly accessible personal journal for an individual. Blogs usually contain links and commentary thereon. Term coined by Peter Merholz (peterme.com). Typically updated daily, blogs often reflect the personality of the author. (v.) To author a Web log.*

Other forms: **Blogger**: (n.) A person who blogs.

What started as a simple venue for personal publishing has evolved into a complex, highly-distributed information sharing phenomenon that threatens to fundamentally change the way we share knowledge.

From a lead-generation perspective, blogs are the perfect viral marketing medium and an excellent way to promote a product or message.

To use blogging to your advantage, you can either focus on getting mentioned on existing blogs managed by other people, or you can set up a company blog of your own. Start your own blog using Blogger.com or Typepad.com. Both of these sites make it very easy to set up and post to a blog.

If you would rather work with existing blogs, recognize that most blogs are content-specific. Take time to target and influence the correct blogs. And it is _all_ about influence; there are no guarantees you'll be mentioned, or that a mention will be a positive one. Because blogging circumvents traditional editors and publishers, you must zero in on influential bloggers and blog posting sites interested in your area and integrate your message into those venues.

Use Blogdex.com and Daypop.com to identify the news outlets to which blogs tend to link. Blogdex.com provides a ranked listing of the most hyperlinked stories within the blogging community. Daypop.com searches 17,000 news sites, weblogs and RSS feeds for current event and breaking news keywords you enter. This makes it easy for you to find out where to focus. Spend a little time with it and you can be a blog-savvy marketer in no time.

Go Door-to-Door

Once the exclusive domain of book peddlers, vacuum manufacturer reps and brush salesman, door-to-door selling might be worth your time to investigate.

Over the years, just about everything has been sold door-to-door. From encyclopedia and vacuum cleaners to tax preparation, lawn care, and meal services, if you're trying to reach consumers, there may be no better way.

One of the key advantages is the amount of control that you get over who is exposed to your message, hears your pitch, or receives your offer. You simply choose to work through the neighborhoods you wish to target, and avoid those that you feel are less qualified.

Selling door-to-door is also cost-effective. Most door-to-door salesmen work on commission. This means that you only have to pay the people who are making sales.

Sure, it's easy enough to walk up and ring a doorbell. But there's a trick to getting them to buy. Instead of selling the actual product at the door all you have to do is sell a "gift certificate" for the product instead.

Keep in mind that you don't have to do the knocking yourself. There are legions of young people—including boy scouts, high school juniors and seniors, and church youth groups—who will gladly sell door to door for you.

Quite often, young people from these organizations are just waiting for you to ask them to help. And their motivations can vary considerably. Some are out looking for a summer job where they can make a few bucks, while others are looking to raise money for the clubs to which they belong or organizations that they support.

With a little experimentation, you'll find that it's not too difficult to transform a team of eager young summer-job employees into a gift certificate selling machine. You can find good leads this way, and you'll feel good knowing that you're helping young people fund their college education or support their clubs.

Target Co-Registrants

You probably already know that "Birds of a feather flock together". But do you take advantage of this fact for your lead generation? Whatever business you're in, make it a habit to look for other businesses that seek to attract the same customers you do. Then partner with them to share leads. For example, if you're a wedding photographer, why not arrange with a florist to let each other know when one of you learns of a couple planning a wedding?

This is a natural for the web. Ask your lead sharing partner if they would let you place an opt-in statement on their e-mail newsletter sign-up page. You should offer the same to them, in return. Prospects that make it to either of your landing pages are in a decision-making frame of mind, and are much more likely to say "Yes!" to receiving information about related services, as well.

This is called co-registration, and it's a proven method of building contact lists quickly and cost-effectively. It's a time-saver for your prospects, too.

Don't have any lead-sharing partners? No problem! There are several online services that exist solely for this purpose. Take a look at any of the following:

- leadfactory.com

- topica.com

- innovationads.com/coregistration.htm

- listopt.com

One note of caution. If you use a co-registration service and they claim that they can provide you with a thousand opt in names in a day or so for pennies a name, your best bet is to run, not walk, away. Co-registration is a good example of a situation in which you get what you pay for.

The going rate for co-registration varies between 25 cents and $1 per lead. If you think this is a lot, consider how much it currently costs you to get leads through other avenues. If you pay $750 to run a small ad in a local newspaper, do you get 750 leads? Not usually.

Syndicate Your Site

"Information *wants* to be free," or so the saying goes. Assuming that's true, why is it that getting through all of the information we seem to need from the Internet costs *so* much of our precious time?!

Enter RSS. RSS stands for "Rich Site Summary" or "Really Simple Syndication". (Just pick the one you prefer. No one else really seems to know for sure—or care—which definition is correct).

All sorts of companies are getting into the RSS act. Some use RSS to deliver articles and article previews to readers who are too busy to browse and dig up the content they are interested in. Others use RSS to alert customers of new products, upcoming events, or sales and promotions.

RSS makes it possible to review a large number of sites in a very short time. This is because with RSS readers (called Aggregators) you only read the sites that have changed since the last time you've read the feed.

RSS is also SPAM-free. Since users do not have to give out their email address in order to receive information via RSS, e-mail inboxes do not get cluttered with un-requested and unwanted information.

For publishers, the bottom line is that RSS permits instant distribution of content updates to consumers. Syndicating headlines is an excellent and cost-effective way of driving traffic to any website that publishes new content regularly. Once a website produces an RSS feed, other sites can very easily syndicate their headlines. Headline aggregation services like Moreover.com power news portals, specialist news search engines and business intelligence services. They also provide news feeds to websites. This gives your content a much wider distribution than would otherwise be possible by relying solely on visitors who already know to come to your site.

To read RSS content, you'll need an "Aggregator". Aggregators are software applications and online sites that periodically read a set of RSS feeds, find the new content, and display a list of the headlines on a single page. Some are programs that you download and install on your computer, and others are online services. Some of the most popular are:

- SharpReader—sharpreader.net
- Rocketinfo—rocketinfo.com
- Bloglines—bloglines.com
- Feed Demon—feeddemon.com
- Wildgrape NewsDesk—wildgrape.net

While not overly difficult, the process of creating an RSS feed is beyond what can be shared in this small space. Do a Google search to find out what you need to do, and read Danny Sullivan's excellent article,

"Making an RSS Feed" here: searchenginewatch.com/sereport/arti-cle.php/2175271

Once you've created a feed, you'll need to promote it. Create an information page about syndicating your headlines. This will make existing visitors aware that your website has an RSS file so they can add it to their news reading applications or even include it on their own websites. This information page will be indexed by regular search engines and can also be submitted to various niche directories. Some of the places you may wish to promote your RSS feed include.

- daypop.com
- feedster.com
- FreeSticky.com
- MagPortal.com
- Moreover.com
- Newsfeeds.com
- NewsIsFree.com
- NewsNow.co.uk
- syndic8.com

Once an RSS file has been included in these sources it is likely to be found by websites, online news portals or news reading applications seeking RSS content.

"MACM": A Model for New Business Development

$$\blacktriangledown$$

INTRODUCTION

Do you have a system for getting new business? No? Tsk, tsk! As sure as sales revenue is the lifeblood of any enterprise, getting new business is the most important aspect of every manager's daily responsibilities. Why leave that to chance?

Selling is systematic. So is marketing. That means that, all other things be equal, prospects will respond to the same messages and selling approaches in the same way, time and time again. Therefore, to develop a steady stream of new business, your goal is to uncover that sequence of messages and actions that lead your prospects to buy. We refer to such a process as a *"business development model."*

There are four elements to INVICTUS *Solutions Group*'s business development model. These are:

1. Core **M**arketing Message

2. Prospect **A**cquisition System

3. Client **C**onversion System, and

4. System Performance **M**easurements

The first element—**Core Marketing Message**—is an absolutely essential first step. Without a clear focus on the value you offer, it is impossible to earn an enduring position in prospects' minds. Like it or not, without an enduring position, any sales you get will be the result of luck or convenience. More on this later.

The next two elements—**Prospect Acquisition** and **Customer Conversion**—are the "guts" of the business development process. It's important to develop customers in two steps. Altogether too many businesses try and take their prospects "all the way" in one fell swoop. Quite often, that's just too much for prospects to swallow, and no sale is made.

The final element of INVICTUS' business development system is **System Measurement**. Continuous monitoring, measurement, testing and analysis of marketing and sales processes is how bad marketing programs become good, and how good ones become great.

Let's take a look at these four elements in a little more detail.

CORE MARKETING MESSAGE

There are five components to consider when developing an effective Core Marketing Message:

- **Target Audience**: *to whom are you speaking?*
- **Problem**: *what issues, pains, predicaments or challenges are your target clients facing?*

- **Solution**: *what results do you produce for clients?*

- **Proof**: *how can you prove that you can deliver that solution?*

- **Differentiation**: *what makes you stand apart from your competitors?*

Address each component as fully and completely as possible and you've got the first stake in the ground as you work toward implementing a business development model that becomes a well-spring of new business, year after year.

Which Target Audience?

The starting point is to answer the question "who should you serve?". Define your ideal target in terms of:

- Industry: *what industry are you targeting?*

- Geography: *what boundaries apply?*

- Company Size: *revenues? employees?*

- Decision-Maker: *who are your ideal sponsors?*

What Problem?

Once you've identified your target audience, you need to develop a rock-solid grip on the specific problems and challenges your prospects face. Ask yourself the following:

- What are the most pressing problems faced by your target audience?

- Who owns the problem?

- How much does it cost to have problems like that?

- How are they currently addressing these problems?

- What alternatives exist?

What Solution?

With the prospect's problem in mind, now consider what you have to offer. Answer the following:

- What do you do to solve the prospect's problem?

- How will your services help your client avoid pain ABC, or achieve benefit XYZ?

- How is your solution better/faster/cheaper than what the prospect is doing now, and any alternatives that are available to them?

- What benefits will prospects realize from letting you work with them to solve their problems?

How Do You Prove It?

Credibility is paramount. Without it, even the most clever marketing messages fall on deaf ears.

Although the need for credibility is pervasive, it is more important in some situations than in others. Take the case of *Experience* goods. These are those in which consumers cannot examine quality attributes before purchase, but can observe quality attributes after purchase. In navigating such a purchase situation, consumers will search for information or cues that can help them gain a level of comfort sufficient to make a purchase decision. This reduces the risk that they will make a wrong decision.

Ways to prove product or service capabilities include:

- Testimonials: *written endorsements from clients*

- Case Studies: *stories of client successes*

- References: *telephone calls and/or site visits*

- Public Relations: *frequent mentions in the media*

How Do You Differentiate Yourself?

As George Orwell might have said, "All marketers are created equal, but some are more equal than others." Why should your prospects choose you? You need to be able to answer the following:

- What makes you unique, special, or memorable?

- What is your true advantage over other firms?

- There are three main points of differentiation:

  - Your Offer: what you do for clients

  - Your Service Delivery: how you do what you do

  - Your Image: the place you hold in clients' minds

With careful reflection, you can weave your answers to the questions above into a marketing message that resonates with your target audience, and sets you up for strong and consistent ***Prospect Acquisition***.

Prospect Acquisition

Prospect Acquisition refers to the identification of a *qualified* prospect who agrees to speak with us *when a suitable opportunity arises* to consider our services.

Yes, those highlighted parts in the previous sentence are important. A *qualified* prospect is one who has the money, authority, and desire to buy. Miss any one of those three elements, and there will be no sale.

It is also prudent to recognize that buyers can like what you offer enough to have decided to buy from you, but not be ready to buy just yet. Buyers pass through a series of stages on their journey from awareness to purchase of any good or service. Consumer behaviorists refer to this as the *Hierarchy of Effects*.

<u>Who Are Your Prospects?</u>
Any discussion of lead generation and prospect acquisition must begin with a discussion about *who* you are trying to attract. It never ceases to amaze me to learn how much time and money business owners and managers will spent to attracting new customers when, in fact, *new* customers are not even the best prospects!

Consider the entire market of prospects for your products or services. Of this market, some are aware of what you offer, and some are not. Some of those that are aware of your offerings have tried you before, and others have not. Further, some of those that have tried you were satisfied, but others were not. If we agree that this is a "typical" market structure, here is the "correct" order in which to target prospects:

1. Entire Market > Those Who Are Aware > Have Tried > Were Satisfied

2. Entire Market > Those Who Are Aware > Have Tried > Were Not Satisfied

3. Entire Market > Those Who Are Aware > Have Not Tried

4. Entire Market > Those Who Are Unaware

Why give so much attention to existing customers? Let me count the ways...

- Existing customers are much more likely to buy from you than are new customers,

- Marketing costs to win new business from existing clients are lower than from new clients,

- Follow-on work for existing customers is often more profitable, and

- For businesses that sell more expensive, customized goods or services, the challenging, firm-expanding projects are the ones that you can only win from clients with whom you have established relationships built on confidence and trust.

Why bother with unhappy customers? If *"because it's the right thing to do"* isn't enough for you, here are some other reasons you might want to consider. For starters, they may be easier to turn around than you think. The "straw that broke the camel's back" may not have been that heavy. Second, turning them around may stop bad word-of-mouth. I'm sure you've heard the statistics about how negative word of mouth can damage a business. If you haven't, here are the cold hard facts: *Satisfied customers tell 5 other people about their good treatment. The average person with a problem eventually tells 9 other people!* Clearly, if you are producing unhappy customers with any regularity, it makes sense to do what you can to stem the flow.

Yet another reason to focus on unhappy customers is because talking to them about what went wrong will help you make your products and services even better. And in today's hyper-competitive business environment, you should be looking incessantly for any way you can improve your operation.

How to Acquire a Prospect

Business development is best done in two steps: **acquiring prospects**, and then **converting them to customers**. Successful marketing is like dating. You wouldn't give a marriage proposal on the first date, would you? It takes time to warm prospects up to your propositions. You have to know, like, and trust each other before you can do business together.

To start the relationship, you want to essentially get prospects to "raise their hands" and tell you that they have an interest in what you have to offer. It is from this second pool of prospects that you will convert your customers.

The easiest way to get those hands raised is to use some sort of bait. Offer a free report, white paper, trial or sample, audit or something that will benefit the customer to inquire. Naturally, only those interested in what you have to sell will take you up on the offer. It is the people in this group that are your best prospects.

Keep these tips in mind if you use advertising to generate leads: The purpose of ads is to sell the bait, not your product or service. Always put a claim or promise in the headline. The headline is responsible for 70% of the response. Talk about how customers will benefit from your services, not about your business.

Advertising is not always the best way to generate leads, however. By definition, ads are blatantly commercial, and often viewed with skepticism. Here are some other ideas for how you might generate that initial attention:

- Create An E-mail Signature That Promotes Your Bait Piece

- Use Community Bulletin Boards

- Send Postcards

- Teach A College Course

- Sponsor A Web Site

- Set Up A Cross Promotion

- Focus On Referrals

- Hand Out Bookmarks

- Send Out Press Releases

- Go To Your Customers' Trade Shows

- Hold A Contest

- Get On The Radio

- Hire A Telemarketer

- Volunteer

A great deal of study has been devoted to developing business for professional services firms. As a general rule, the two most successful business development activities for professional services firms are speaking (specifically keynote addresses and small-scale seminars) and writing articles, research reports, and books. The next-best activities include:

- Actively Seeking Referrals from Current and Past Clients,

- Community/Civic Activities,

- Networking with Potential Clients, and

- Keep-in-Touch Activities *(i.e. e-mail & printed newsletters)*

After these fundamentals come everything else a professional services firm might think of to try and get attention in the marketplace. There are many things you might try but, at the end of the day, they are simply not as effective as the items described above. (For more on this, buy and read a copy of David Maister's seminal work, _Managing the Professional Services Firm_.)

Whatever tactics you use, remember that you must accomplish two objectives:

1. Educating & Informing _(Develop prospects' trust in our abilities)_

2. Relationship-Building _(Make prospects comfortable working with us)_

Remember: all you are trying to do in the Prospect Acquisition stage is get prospects to _"raise their hands"_. Once those hands are in the air, it's time to move on to **Customer Conversion**. This is where the rubber hits the road. This is where business _lives_. Most importantly for your business, perhaps, this is where people give you money.

Of course, what we're talking about is sales. This article will not attempt to lay out a "one-size-fits-all" framework for effective sales. It will, however, provide a framework within which sales can be effective. In fact, without such a framework, consistently _profitable_ sales are simply not likely.

Customer Conversion

Customer Conversion refers to the process and tactics employed to get a prospect to buy our goods or services. While the discussion in this Brief emphasizes account-based sales such as one would find in technology or professional services firms, many of the principles hold true for other industries and business organizations as well.

Recall from our previous discussion that, in most cases, the best source of new projects is *existing customers*. Why do we emphasize existing customers? Let me remind you of some of the reasons:

- Existing clients are much more likely to buy than new clients;

- Marketing costs to win new business from existing clients are lower than from new clients;

- Follow-on projects are often more profitable; and

- The challenging, firm-expanding projects are the ones that you can only win from clients with whom you have established relationships built on confidence and trust.

Assuming you've followed that advice and are ready to move on to some customer-base expanding activities, let's take a look at how to bring a few new customers into the fold.

The first question to ask yourself is, "from the prospects I've developed through my **Prospect Acquisition** activities, *which accounts are most worth penetrating?*" As George Orwell might have advised, "*all customers are created equal, but some are more equal than others.*"

What you want to look for are those prospects that are most aligned with what you have to offer. Which offer the greatest long-term profitability potential?

(Don't know how to find them? Okay, okay...here's a leg up: send me an e-mail and I'll send you a spreadsheet to help you calculate the life-time value of your customers.)

Once you've selected an account to pursue, you should establish a budget for your conversion initiative. How much can you afford to spend, in order to bring this customer on board? Consider both out-of-pocket expenses & cost of time committed. Proceeding without considering your cost of sales can lead you down a very unprofitable black hole.

Keep in mind, however, that it's not uncommon for businesses to spend more on acquiring and converting a customer than they recover in the first sale or even the first few sales they make to that customer. Customer acquisition and conversion is best viewed as an investment in the long-run viability of your business.

With your budget in mind, design and execute a client-specific sales and marketing campaign. Your goal is to convert prospects to customers as efficiently as possible (read: "efficient=CHEAP!").

There's an important note to be made, here. A wise man once said, "*I know that half of all the money I spend on advertising is wasted. I just don't know which half.*" Don't let this be you. Through all of your acquisition and conversion activities, do yourself a favor and measure, measure, measure the effectiveness of everything you do!

It never ceases to amaze me how, time after time, most managers and small business owners spend a great deal of time, money and effort learning to sell (i.e. convincing people of the value of what they have to offer), and dedicate virtually no time studying how people buy. Here's a quick introduction to how people buy. It's called the ***"PIED-P"* Buying Process**, and it's the steps we all follow, whenever we buy anything. Sure, we short-cut the process for routine, low-value and low-risk purchases. But it is impossible for us to buy without taking these steps.

1. **Problem Recognition**—we sense a need to solve some "problem," be it hunger, the need for transportation, or a replacement for a crashed computer

2. **Identification of Alternatives**—we look for ways to solve our problem

3. **Evaluation of Alternatives**—we consider our options

4. **Decision**—we choose, and we buy

5. **Post-purchase Decision**—the confirmation or condemnation of the appropriateness of decision we just made (this is also our opportunity for "cognitive dissonance"—that nagging feeling we sometimes get that makes us wonder if we've done the right thing, to after we've made a big decision)

The key to customer conversion is to figure out how *your* customers buy, and then systematically lower or eliminate the barriers that sometimes keep them from doing so. Where are they, and what are they usually doing when they realize they have a problem that needs to be solved? Where do they look for relief? What specific attributes do they look at as they compare alternative solutions and solutions providers? How do they ultimately decide? These are the questions to ask and answer, as you seek to put in place consistently effective customer conversion processes.

As you develop your plans, keep in mind these fundamental Laws of New Client Marketing:

- "Raspberry Jam Rule"—*The Wider You Spread It, the Thinner It Gets.*

- Marketing Works When It Demonstrates, Not When It Asserts.

- In-person Tactics Are More Effective Than Written-word Tactics.

- Marketing Is a Seduction, Not an Assault.

System Performance Measurement

Marketing measurement is tough. Accurate marketing measurement is even tougher. But it's something that you simply must do. Without a consistent approach to analyzing the effectiveness of your business development efforts, however, it's a certainty that you're throwing some of your money away.

Although the exact mix of appropriate measurements varies with different types of enterprises, here are a few you might want to consider as you plan how to measure the effectiveness of your Prospect Acquisition and Customer Conversion activities.

Prospect Acquisition Measures

Inquiries by Media Source

- <u>What This Measure Means</u>—This measure refers to the number of people who "raised their hand" and responded to your offer for each promotional approach employed.

- <u>Why You Might Want To Measure This</u>—It is important to segment this number by the individual media used in order to evaluate the effectiveness of each media channel. This permits a comparison of the number and percent response between lists, publications, etc.

Cold Call Yield

- <u>What This Measure Means</u>—The number of cold calls required to turn up one prospect interested in what you have to offer.

- <u>Why You Might Want To Measure This</u>—If cold calling is an effective lead generation technique for your business, this number will help you calculate how scaling up your cold calling operation will affect the total number of leads generated in a given period of time. In other words, if one cold-caller can turn up two solid leads each day, then five managed just as effectively should turn up 10 leads.

Cost per Acquired Lead

- <u>What This Measure Means</u>—The cost for each lead generated. To calculate this, divide the total cost of a lead generation campaign by the number of leads produced.

- <u>Why You Might Want To Measure This</u>—It permits a comparison of costs for each effort and allows you to know for future marketing plans whether the media was cost effective. It's possible you may receive the lowest cost per inquiry or conversion, but it may have originated from the media with the highest cost per thousand. In other words, the media that *cost the most* may not be the *most expensive*.

Time to Lead

- <u>What This Measure Means</u>—Measure of the time lapse between when the prospect was exposed to the marketing message and when they "raised their hand" to indicate their interest.

- <u>Why You Might Want To Measure This</u>—This time lapse is an important part of calculating the total time needed to generate a new client. When combined with *Sales Cycle Time* (see below), this give you an idea of how long it currently takes you to generate a new client "from scratch".

Customer Conversion Measures

Conversions by Media Source

- <u>What This Measure Means</u>—The number of customers who buy from you, sorted by media source.

- <u>Why You Might Want To Measure This</u>—Helps you compare the total number of sales created and percent response between contact methods.

Cost per Converted Sale

- <u>What This Measure Means</u>—The cost for each lead converted to a sale. Simply add up all costs of a lead generation campaign, and divide by the number of new sales.

- <u>Why You Might Want To Measure This</u>—It permits a comparison of costs for each effort and allows you to know for future marketing plans whether the media was cost effective. Cost per conversion is one of the most important numbers you can calculate. It's possible for one media to have a low number of leads (with a high cost per lead), but a very high conversion rate bringing down the overall marketing cost per sale.

Profit and Return on Investment

- <u>What This Measure Means</u>—The final score card. Reveals how much every dollar spent on marketing costs returned in profit.

- <u>Why You Might Want To Measure This</u>—It enables you justify expenditures and determine if the marketing program made sense.

Sales Cycle Time

- <u>What This Measure Means</u>—The length of time between when a prospect is first identified and when that prospect becomes a customer.

- <u>Why You Might Want To Measure This</u>—This is an essential number when planning cash flow and evaluating business risk.

One quick note about tracking leads and conversions by media source. Wherever possible, do not rely on self-reported lead source (asking the prospect to tell you how they heard about you). This is seldom effective, as prospects may have heard about or seen your messages in several places before deciding to act. What you're most interested in is the promotion or advertisement that caused them to act *now*. Therefore, put in place mechanisms to track prospects whether or not they tell you where they heard about you.

To do this, you want to channel their response from each media into defined paths. For example, you might run a promotional contest and advertise using TV ads, postcard campaign, and Internet banner ads. The TV ad may encourage prospects to go to the following web site:

yourcompany/2004contest.htm. The postcard campaign might use yourcompany.com/04contest.htm. And the banner ads may point to yourcompany.com/contest2004.htm. Only you will know which medium directed prospects to which page, and you won't have to rely on prospects to remember and then accurately tell you how they heard about you.

About INVICTUS
Solutions Group

— ▼ —

INVICTUS *Solutions Group* is an executive advisory practice that helps organizations get more customers, more quickly, at less cost.

INVICTUS helps organizations analyze the motives of the buying decision and construct customer profiles to identify the most likely buyers. We look at current and past customers, determine which are the most profitable, research their buying behavior and develop a profile, and put in place mechanisms to attract and do business with them, and those most like them. Although we have worked with clients in many different industries, the majority of our engagements are with technology sales organizations and professional services firms.

Our business development services span five main areas:

Service Area	We Answer Questions Such As
Market Assessment	• *Which markets or market segments bear the most fruit, and what are the challenges in reaching them?* • *What problems are experienced most consistently by customers in the market segments we have selected?* • *Who is my competition, and how can I make my offerings stand out in my customers' minds?* • *How do customers choose? What factors do they consider, and how much importance do they place on each factor?*
Value Refinement	• *How can I bundle or package my offerings in order to provide even more value for the customers I serve?* • *Am I asking enough for what I provide to customers? Am I charging too much?* • *Are there any follow-on products or services I can offer customers to sustain our relationship?* • *What other organizations might want to partner with me to develop a combined offering to our mutual customers?*
Go-to-Market Strategy	• *How do I get the word out about our products and services quickly and cost-effectively?* • *What should I say to get new customers coming in droves, and what could I say that might keep them away?* • *Which messages will be most effective in helping customers understand why they should do business with our firm?* • *How do I "get in the way" of customers already motivated to look for the products and services I offer?*

Service Area	We Answer Questions Such As
Communications Programming	• *How do customers want to buy: From resellers? At a retail location? Online? Through a direct sales force?* • *How can I help my sales force get a greater number of better-qualified leads to follow?* • *Where do I find the right agents, distributors, resellers, or OEM partners and how do I get them to carry my products?* • *What can I do to prevent channel conflict between my sales force and our distribution partners?*
Customer Loyalty & Retention	• *Why do my customers buy from me?* • *How do I turn my customers into "Customer Evangelists" for my company, and refer other people to my company?* • *How do I make a greater number of my customers more satisfied, more often?* • *How do I keep my best customers coming back for more, and encourage them to try my other products or services?*

About the Author

▼

Robin C. Johnston is Director of INVICTUS *Solutions Group*. A serial entrepreneur and a seasoned sales & marketing pro, Robin excels at developing marketing and business development plans, generating leads, deploying programs to out-market competitors, and accelerating revenue with limited marketing budgets. He developed the senior-year Internet Marketing course currently used at the University of North Carolina's Charlotte campus, and has held faculty and management positions at Randolph Community College in Asheboro, North Carolina and Clarke College in Ontario, Canada. Audiences delight in Robin's ability to integrate marketing and sales principles from a variety of industries, and convey marketing skills in an accessible, humorous and powerful manner.

Robin has spent his entire career helping companies improve marketing and increase sales. Before founding INVICTUS in 2002, Robin led the marketing team for a well-known enterprise spend management software company. His team drove the leads that grew the company from start-up to 90 people in just 18 months.

Robin has earned the Certified Management Consultant designation, the highest designation bestowed by the Institute of Management Consultants. He also holds an MBA in Marketing and Corporate Strategy.

INVICTUS *Solutions Group*
www.INVICTUSsolutions.com

Contact us to discuss how you can get more business for your business!

INVICTUS *Solutions Group*   E-Mail: info@INVICTUSsolutions.com
WWW: http://www.INVICTUSsolutions.com

Index

978-0-595-38723-6
0-595-38723-3

www.ingramcontent.com/pod-product-compliance
Lightning Source LLC
Chambersburg PA
CBHW031053180526
45163CB00002BA/819